Teaching of Commerce

Published by
Saurabh Publishing House

TEACHING OF COMMERCE

Seema Kaur

Saurabh
Publishing House
4263/3, Ansari Road,
Darya Ganj, New Delhi-110002

Published by :
SAURABH PUBLISHING HOUSE

Distributed by :
LOTUS PRESS
4263/3, Ansari Road, Darya Ganj, New Delhi-110002
Ph : 32903912, 23280047 • E-Mail : lotus_press@sify.com

Saurabh Publishing is an imprint of
Lotus Press

Teaching of Commerce

ISBN : 978-81-89005-45-0 (H/B)

Printed in India by Anand Sons, Delhi.

Preface

Commerce or Business Education is just one phase of education, not inferior or superior to any other phase or branch. The increasing complexity of business and commerce organisations in the present day world has made it obligatory for students to be conversant with modern principles and practices of management and accounting. Gone are the days when one could depend on the '*Munims*' and their '*Bahi Khatas*'. The use of computers and the management techniques of the behavioural sciences have completely revolutionised the running of modern business and commercial enterprises. Therefore, it has become very necessary to pay adequate attention to Business and Commerce Education.

This book deals with the topics of—*Introduction to Teaching of Commerce; Teaching Technique; Requirement for Commerce Teacher; Curriculum in Commerce; Teaching Methods of Commerce; Audio-Visual Aids; Importance of Text-Book; Teaching Competency in Commerce; Evaluation Principles in Commerce; Methods of Teaching Accountancy; Teaching of Final Accounts; Instructor and Lesson Planning* etc.

I hope that students and those in the administration field will find it useful for academic and competitive examinations. I owe a deep sense of gratitude to my publisher for materialising my present endeavour.

Author

Contents

1

Introduction to Teaching of Commerce

One may adopt the expression 'Commerce Education' as the generic name to cover all types and levels of education for all the business functions or operations, whether in the public or private sector, except those directly involved in the mechanical extraction or transformation of materials to products and maintenance of machines. The expressions 'Commercial Education', 'Commerce Education' and 'Professional Business Education' may be used to indicate three levels of 'Business Education'—the first to cover the junior level programmes, the second to mean the first degree programmes, and the third to cover all post-graduate and post-employment specialist or expert level programmes. The general business knowledge may be integrated within the general education programmes. Marginal Business Education can be included within the other specific programmes and need not be covered by the Business Education programmes proper. The programmes in Business Education proper at different levels should be such as may serve the needs of both the public and the private sectors of the economy, as also the need of the owner-enterprisers and of the employee-managers. The direction of economic development that the country has adopted seems to suggest that the difference between the two groups or sectors would gradually close up the individual for effective participation as a citizen and consumer in the Indian society.

Definitions of Commerce Education

According to *Freok Hooper* and *James Graham*, "A practical education suited to the needs of present day, and calculated to fit young people intended for business careers for work they will have to perform and to better equip for their work those already in business."

According to *Leveret S. Lyon* Commerce Education is "any education which a businessman has and which makes him a better businessman, is for him a business education, no matter whether it was obtained in the walls of a school or not."

According to *Chessman A. Herrick*, "that form of instruction that both directly and indirectly prepares the businessman for his calling."

Paul S. Lomax states that, "Commercial Education is fundamentally a programme of economic education that has to do with the requirement, conservation and spending of wealth."

According to *H.G. Shields*, "Real Commerce Education is Economic Education not of academic sort long on theory and short on facts but Economic Education which will give the student a knowledge of basic reality of business life and relationships. The basic science of business is commerce and without a thorough guidance and awareness of economic problems much of the material included in secondary school course is purely additive and essentially superficial.

Fredrick G. Nichols said, "Commercial education is a type of training which, while playing its part in the achievement of the general aims of education of any given level, has for its primary objective the preparation of people to enter upon a business career, or having entered upon such a career, to render more efficient service therein and to advance from their present levels of employment to higher levels".

R.E. Tonne said, "If education is thought of as the adjustment of the individual to his environment, Business Education must be thought of as the adjustment of the individual to his business environment."

According to Policies Commission on Business and Economic Education Statement, "Business Education represents a broad and diverse discipline that is included in all types of educational delivery systems—elementary and secondary schools, one and two-year schools and colleges, and five-year colleges and universities. Business Education can begin at any level; it can be interpreted for varying periods of time, and it can be continued throughout life span of an individual. Business Education includes education for office occupations, distribution and marketing occupations, business teaching, business administration, and economic undertakings."

Calhour states that, "Business Education is interpreted in many ways. To some, it pertains only to those occupations that are carried out in the office by office workers. Others interpret its scope to include not only the jobs performed by office workers but also the functions by management and/or advancement in occupations related to the office. In addition, business education provides the student with the understanding and knowledge needed for handling personal affairs and using the service of the business world."

Vocational Education

Defining business of economic organisation, "chiefly for gratifying human wants," some writers have identified the term "Business Education" with all Vocational Education. But such an approach seems to be too broad for evolving programmes in Business Education, although it is admitted that, "Business Education can make some contribution to the training of all workers." The coverage of Vocational Education is broader, and Business Education can be only one branch of Vocational Education if the term vocation is understood in a broad sense.

Economic Education

Some writers have asserted that, "real Business Education is Economic Education—Economic Education not of academic sort, long on theory and short on facts—but Economic Education which will give the students a knowledge of basic realities of business life and relationships". Such identification of Business Education with education in applied Economic or Social Science is found in many countries at the university level. The German concept of "Enterprise economics" is based on such idea. But then, different branches of knowledge like law, cost accountancy, etc., are brought within the domain. In Britain, the majority of the Carr-Saunders Committee recommended the Applied Economics and Social Science approach in this branch of education at university level. In Switzerland, the name is 'commercial Science', presumably to widen the coverage on the argument of scientific study.

Management Education

In the U.S.A. Business Education at university level is being identified with "Management Education" or "Business Administration", and Business Education at less than the college level is being intended to be covered by "Vocational Business Education" and similar other terms. The Harvard programmes are claimed to mark a break away from the applied economics approach in higher business education. Another British writer *A.B. Lowndes* states that "the whole programme of commercial teaching then aims at the provision of training for the whole of the commercial and administrative aspects of industry, and not only for the narrower aspects of buying-selling, banking, transporting, warehousing, and recording."

Nature of Commerce Education

1. An Integrated Subject. The Scottish Education Department in its booklet on the commercial subjects in secondary schools, stresses that "the function of Commercial Education is not merely to satisfy the vocational need of the pupils but also to foster an understanding of the economy of the community in which they will be called to play a part. In commerce no less than in industry, it is of primary importance that prospective entrants should have a sound general education." In his pamphlet on "Commercial Studies in Secondary Schools" Mr. Graham Savage of the London Country Council explains that "the essential function of a secondary school commercial course should be to give the pupils a knowledge of the background of commerce and of the way it affects the life of the community; the pupil's interest in commerce cannot, therefore, be confined to subjects which are specially commercial, but will influence their approach to other subjects." The commercial curriculum in secondary education in Switzerland and Norway, include sufficient number of the so-called general subjects.

About this integration approach to the liberal and vocational education, Prof. Whitehead observes in his book "*The Aims of Education*" and other Essays that "the antithesis between the technical and liberal education is fallacious. There can be no adequate technical education which is not liberal, and no liberal education which is not technical; that is, no education which does not impart both technique and intellectual vision. In simple language, education should turn the people to something he knows well and can do well. This intimate union of practice and theory aids both. The intellect does not work best in vacuum." The Mudaliar Commission rightly stressed, "that the intellectual and cultural development of different individuals take place best through a variety of media, that the book or the study of traditional academic subjects is not the only door to the education of the personality and that, in the case of many-perhaps the majority of the children, practical work intelligently organised can unlock their latent energies much more successfully than the traditional subjects which address themselves only to the mind, or worse still, the memory". The Commissioners for Secondary Education in Britain observed that, "all education is development and discipline of faculty by the communication of knowledge and whether the faculty may be eye or hand or the reason and imagination and whether the knowledge be so communicated as evoke and exercise a disciplined faculty, the process is rightly termed education."

2. Both a Knowledge Subject and a Skill Subject. The objectives of the study of commerce are both preparatory to further studies in colleges or high education and terminal to enter into the careers of middle level lines of employment.

3. Both Academic and Vocational. Thus, Commerce is both an academic discipline and a vocational subject.

In the U.S.A., Business Education is not meant to cover technical or technological education for industry. In both U.K. and U.S.A., as also elsewhere, industrial organisation and management, industrial economics etc. are considered business or commercial subjects.

Scope of Commerce Education

The Special Committee on Education for Commerce in Britain thus, delimited the coverage of Commerce Education: "Education for Commerce must therefore embrace educational facilities for those preparing for or engaged in business occupations of every kind, professional or otherwise, from office routine such as typewriting and shorthand to the positions of great responsibility.... It is in the sense that we understand the breadth of our enquiry; it includes education for wholesale and retail trade, for import and export trade, for transport and shipping, for general commerce, for profession so-called, for higher functions of management and administration, and for the move modest 'hand-maidens' of commerce, shorthand and typewriting."

Scope of Commerce Education has changed radically during the past six decades. *Abbot-Wood* Report said about Commerce Education.

"This branch (Education for Commerce) of vocational education differs so greatly from education for industry, that it demands separate consideration. It must be so framed as to meet the needs of both the two main groups into which we have divided workers in commercial occupations, that is, *(a)* of the group of which the members have the responsibility for transacting business on an important scale or for performing the professional functions of banking, accountancy and the like, and *(b)* of the very large group engaged in recording the transactions of the member of the first group".

Scope at College Level

According to the University Education Commission 1948-49, Professional Business Education should include mathematics, statistics; theory of organisation; business structure; finance, including management and budgeting of assets and of expenses; philosophy, history and theory of law; and organisation of work, including economy, process analysis and procedures, standardisation of skills, cost analysis, and the like. The structure of distribution should also be studied. In industrial cases this training can be slanted towards factory practice, office management; institutional management, agriculture, or marketing, according to the student's chief interest. While industrial relations should be included in every business course it is so important as to constitute a profession of itself.

Scope at the Senior Secondary Stage

The Central Board of Secondary Education, Delhi (1996) has outlined the following subject-matter in Business Studies and Accountancy, the terms used by it in lieu of Commerce.

A. Business Studies

(i) Economic Activities and Business

(ii) Nature and Purpose of Business

(iii) Structure of Business

(iv) Forms of Business Enterprise

(v) Service Sector and Business

(vi) Corporate Organisation

(vii) Sources of Business Finance

(viii) Formation of a Company

(ix) Stock Exchange

(x) Internal Trade

B. Accountancy

(i) Accounting—Meaning, Objectives and Basic Accounting Terms

(ii) Theory Base of Accounting

(iii) Origin and Recording of Functions

(iv) Financial Statements—Trading Account Profit

(v) Trial Balance and Errors

(vi) Computer Awareness

(vii) Loss Account and Business sheet

(viii) Depreciation, Reserves and Provision

(ix) Bills of Exchange

(x) Accounts of Non-profit Organisations

As an academic discipline and a vocational discipline Commerce Education includes the following subjects at the senior secondary stage:

1. Business Studies
2. Book Keeping and Accountancy
3. Applied Economics
4. Advertising and Publicity, etc.
5. Commercial English
6. Commercial Law
7. Commercial Mathematics
8. Office, Clerical and Secretarial Practice
9. Salesmanship
10. Shorthand
11. Typewriting
12. Computer Education

Objectives of Teaching Commerce

In their joint work "Principles and Problems of Business Education" *G.K. Hayden* and *C.A. Nolson* have laid down the following objectives :

A. Vocational competency,

B. Adaptability to occupational change.

A. Vocational Competency

Initially only two subjects were included (*viz.*, stenography and book-keeping) Private institutions were already imparting education in these fields. The text-books and material used by such institution were adopted to a large extent.

At present, Vocational competency is not the only objective of Commerce Education. Several other objectives have been added. The number of subjects being taught has increased.

1. Elements of Commerce

In view:

(i) To make students understand the importance of nature of trade and activities in trade, commerce and business.

(ii) To develop various fundamental principles of economic implications of business investments so that they may understand as to how to do business and how to make investments in business and trade.

(iii) To enahle students to undertake various banking activities.

(iv) To enable students to appreciate the organisation and business organisation.

(v) To make students understand about transportation, information and broadcasting and to understand as to how do they benefit individuals, the society and the nation.

(vi) To develop students' capacity to appreciate the services rendered national and international trade and commerce.

(vii) To appreciate the activities of the various instruments of business credits adopted by business houses.

(viii) To provide the students with some background information that may help them in their effort on

studying vocational knowledge and techniques of applying them in business.

(ix) To provide the students with such experiences that enable them in understanding the economic relations of the world and become intelligent participant in community and national affairs.

(x) To develop in students thy skills in preparing notes and drafts of official activities.

(xi) To help students to develop skills of organising and managing different business machinaries so that they may be able to acquaint themselves with routine of the office.

(xii) To enable the students to be able to serve in various sectors of trade, commerce and business.

(xiii) To develop students' knowledge about various business practices and procedurals.

(xiv) To help the students to prosecute their higher education with better and complex skills needed at that stage.

2. Commercial Geography

(i) To help the students in understanding the economic world and to acquaint them with various national and artificial resources available to the mankind.

(ii) To try to make clear to the students that "man is the product of the environment".

(iii) To make them understand the increasing interdependence of people in their social inter-relationship.

(iv) To develop appreciation of the local, regional and world geographic influence upon the life of individuals and nations.

(v) To encourage the students to appreciate the habits, manners, customs, cultures of the people living in different regions.

(vi) To tell the students about the inter-relationship of geography factors and technological developments.

(vii) To make clear to the students the relationship that exits between geography and commerce.

3. Economics

(i) To develop economic understanding.

(ii) To develop students understanding of economic problems and their effects on society.

(iii) To make clear to the students the effects of are individuals economic activities upon the social welfare and a sense of responsibility for improving the social welfare.

(iv) To develop sense of values that serve as the basis of economic planning.

(v) To bring home to the students the effects of the activities of consumer and producer upon economic system.

(vi) To help the students to determine a proper balance between savings and expenditure

(vii) To promote understanding of the means of raising the standard of living.

(viii) To promote understanding of means if raising opportunities of employment.

(ix) To promote the means of checking the exploitation of labour.

(x) To provide knowledge of various means for increasing per capita income.

4. Book-keeping and Accountancy

(a) Primary Vocational Objective. It requires that the learner should be able to take up the job of an accountant/accounts clerk/accounts assistant in some business organisation, Government Department. The teaching of book-keeping and accountancy aims at equipping the pupil to do the job. It is also helpful to those who work in related fields such as store-keepers, cashiers purchase assistants etc.

(b) Personal Use Objective. The pupil may study the subject only for personal use and not for any career. It is useful for doctors, lawyers etc. keeping their accounts for their own purposes.

(c) General Education Objective

(i) Develops in the pupil a habit for neat, clean and methodical work.

(ii) Makes clear to the pupil the need for maintaining systematic records in the management of personal, family, institutional and commercial business affairs.

(iii) Helps in developing good business habits.

(iv) Develops a better understanding of business principles and business practices through the study of business transactions and their effects on business operations.

(v) Provides an opportunity to the students, "to explore and try out experiences in record keeping and interpretation and help them in determining their interest and aptitude for

book-keeping or any other business work as a vocation.

(vi) Provides vocational training to interested students and helps them to qualify for Book-keeping and Accountancy positions.

Objectives as at Pennsylvania Department of Public Instructions

(i) An understanding of the property rights of the proprietor, debtor and creditor.

(ii) An application of the principles of Double-entry system of Book-keeping.

(iii) An understanding of the theory of credits and debits.

(iv) Preparation of the simple form of a Balance-sheet and profit and loss account.

(v) A general understanding of business activities and practices.

(vi) A Knowledge of basic terms such as assets, liabilities, income and expense.

(vii) Mastery of the techniques in olved in performing clerical skills related to Book-keeping.

(viii) Mastery of Technique necessary to keep a simple· set of book for a sole proprietor.

Adaptability to Vocational Changes

Dr. Khan points out, "while inflation increases the opportunity of job of office workers, depression throws out, many a persons, out a job and compels them to find new occupations, Legislation passed by central or state legislatures may create new occupation or may eliminate the existing ones. For example, Income tax act, Sales tax act, etc. have increased the opportunity and also compel the people to change professions. If a good commerce teacher finds that there are no opportunities for promotion due to availability of senior persons may be compelled to change the promotion so that he may get the promotion". A professional should adapt himself to the changes that take place.

Techniques for Development of Attitudes

In vocational subjects, development of attitudes has greater importance than that in the formal academic schemes. In terms of psychology, attitudes stand for either tendency to acquire or avoid. The learner is required to fix up his attitudes in a skill so that he is able to use it in job performance. *Dr. Khan* observes, "Understanding and applications were more important and difficult to teach than knowledge and skills. But teaching of attitudes and ideals was more difficult than teaching of understanding and application. If the teacher is able to develop proper attitudes towards work in particular and life in general, there would be no need for any more teaching to the students. Attitudes cannot be taught directly with any effect. Direct teaching and that too in the form of lecture does not prove much effective in teaching facts, skill, understanding and application but it proves completely useless in teaching of attitudes and ideas".

1. Imitation. Attitude development requires that the teacher should set a good example before the students. He should be punctual in his class to develop proper attitude towards punctuality. To develop proper attitude towards work the teacher should concentrate fully in his period. It is likely develop a proper attitude towards honesty. *Cronbach* a psychologist, says, "An attitude consists of meaning that one associates with a certain object (or abstraction) and that influences has acceptance of it". For development of proper attitudes amongst his students a teacher should himself be adequately competent in those attitudes in which he Wishes to achieve further learning.

2. Learning Activities. According to *Dr. Khan*, "Teacher of facts and skill understanding and appreciation provide the basis of developing attitudes. When we behave with a student in a certain situation, we set a standard for the student and if we have a capacity to live upto the standard we can encourage a standard of behaviour. For example, if we demonstrate discourtesy towards poor handwriting in book-keeping and accountancy we teach and help to develop proper attitude towards good handwriting".

It has been pointed out, "thus through learning activity, the training of attitude development is provided. The role playing is class In respect of the skills also help in development of attitudes.

Functions of Instructional Objectives in Commerce

1. To provide the desired 'directions' of instructional activities involved in the teaching-learning of commerce.
2. To determine the nature of instructional activities.
3. To provide a basis for systematising or planning an instructional programme.
4. To decide on points of emphasis in an instructional activity.
5. To give unity and coherence to an instructional programme.
6. To provide the basis for the measurement growth and thus guard valid evaluation.
7. To help distinguish between various aspects of learning.
8. To help focus attention on proper attributes of teaching and leaning.

9. To help grade learning experiences.
10. To help maintain a balance between different aspects of an instructional programme.
11. To help fix priorities in an instructional programme.
12. To guide instructional decision in curricular and co-curricular areas.
13. To guide in the selection of relevant content.
14. To help make learning functional.
15. To help make the intangibles in instruction tangible.
16. To help identify weaknesses and strengths of pupils in learning.
17. To give meaning to and clarify the structure and content of curriculum.
18. To help articulate learning at various levels.
19. To help discover and evolve properly learning situations.
20. To help define instructional process.
21. To facilitate communication among instructional workers.
22. To guide improvements in instruction.

CBSE Objectives of Teaching Commerce at the Class XI and XII in India

The Central Board of Secondary Education (CBSE) has listed the following objectives of teaching commerce (Business Studies and Accountancy) at the Senior Secondary Stage:

1. To develop in the students an interest in the theory and practice in business, trade and industry.

2. To acquaint students with the theoretical foundations and practices of organising, managing and handling routine operations of a business firm.

3. To inculcate attitudes and values leading to the integration of business with the social system with a positive approach.

4. To equip the students with basic information on modern methods of office operations for effectively carrying out paper work in a business office.

5. To enable students to apply the principles and functions of management to specifIc aspects of business.

6. To generate and promote awareness of students in modern techniques of maintaining accounting records with the help of computers.

7. To impart knowledge of methods considered useful in maintaining records of proprietory and partnership firm companies and non-trading organisations.

7. To equip the students with essential fundamental knowledge for setting-up, organising and handling routine operations of a Small Scale factory.

9. To enable the students to analyse financial statements and interpret the results for decision-making.

10. To create an awareness of the necessity of auditing the detection/rectification of errors/frauds in the process of accounting.

11. To acquaint the students with practice and procedure of determination of cost from the point of its elements.

Objectives of Teaching Commerce at the College Stage

Regarding the nature of Commerce as a discipline The Curriculum Development Centre in Commerce of the University Grants Commission in 1989 made these observations, "Commerce as a discipline is not properly understood by administrators, common men and even by educationists. This is being equated with one subject like Physics or Chemistry or Maths or History etc. In the university system, by and large, there is only one Department of Commerce while under Science discipline that are Departments of Physics, Chemistry, Botany, Biology and so on. There is an urgent need to treat Commerce Discipline at par with Science for its proper development and growth."

The UGC Curriculum Development Centre in Commerce has divided the Commerce Discipline into three major areas : Accounting, Business Studies and Business Economics.

The Centre has suggested the objectives of teaching Commerce at various stages as under.

B.Com. (Hons) I Year

1. To acquaint students with the fundamentals of business organisation and management as a body of knowledge.
2. To impart to the students basic knowledge of important laws applicable to business, trade and industry.
3. To acquaint the students with principles of Business Economics.
4. To provide knowledge to the students of accounting principles and their application in different situations.
5. To develop in the students basic mathematical skills and provide an awareness of computer applications.

6. To provide the students a general understanding of the various aspects of business environment of the country.

7. To develop the ability of the students to communicate clearly and correctly in English and also in the regional languages on matters relevant to day-to-day business operations with emphasis on quality of presentation.

B. Com. (Hons) II Year

1. To provide knowledge and develop skills in the construction of accounts of companies and specialised business entities.

2. To make the students familiar with the basic production process and make them understand the dimensions of production function.

3. To impart knowledge of the application of money in the modern context and monetary theories systems and policies including national income.

4. To familiarise the students with the finance function and acquaint them with working knowledge of various techniques of financial decision-making.

5. To acquaint students with the techniques of statistical measures and analysis.

B.Com. (Hons) III Year

1. To provide an understanding of the main provisions of Income Tax Acts, and their application.

2. To impart knowledge of the principles, methods and techniques of auditing and their application.

3. To provide an insight into the concepts, theories, agreements and regulatory framework relating to

international trade, and to expose the students to the contemporary problems in the area.

4. To impart knowledge and understanding of various aspects of personal policies, problems and management.

5. To impart knowledge of various aspects of marketing and acquaint the students with the applied problems of marketing, with special reference to India.

6. To impart knowledge of the concept and theories of public finance and their application in India.

B. Com. (Professional) I Year

1. To acquaint the students with the fundamentals of business organisation and management as a body of knowledge.

2. To impart to the students basic knowledge of important laws applicable to business, trade and industry.

3. To acquaint the students with principles of business economics.

4. To provide knowledge of accounting principles and their application in different business situations.

5. To provide a general understanding of the various aspects of business environment of the country.

6. To develop basic mathematical skills and provide an awareness of computer applications.

7. To develop ability to communicate clearly and correctly in English and also in the regional languages, on matters relevant to day-to-day business operations with emphasis on quality of presentation.

B. Com. (Professional) II Year

1. To acquaint the students with the basic concepts and tools used in cost accounting management control.
2. To make students conversant with the local environment in which the small business units and other professions operate and to familiarise them with their special accounting requirements.
3. To familiarise the students with the finance function and acquaint them with working knowledge of various techniques of financial decision-making.
4. To acquaint the students with practical and operational problems relating to factory organisation and operational management.
5. To acquaint students with the techniques of statistical measures and analysis.
6. To familiarise students with the organisation and functioning of various bank and non-bank institutions in the money and capital market of India.

B. Com. (Professional) III Year (Accounting)

1. To provide students with the knowledge of some higher aspects and problems of company accounts.
2. To create among students an awareness of the potentialities of electronic data processing in various stages of cost recording, ascertainment, and improvement. They are to use computer as a working tool for preparing budgets and other accounts through cobol programming.
3. To make students conversant with the taxation system and to provide detailed knowledge of customs and central excise duties in India.

4. To impart knowledge of the principles, methods and techniques of auditing and their application.

5. To provide an understanding of the main provisions of Income Tax Acts, and their applications.

6. To prepare students for practising in the Wealth Tax, Gift Tax and Sales Tax etc.

B. Com. (Professional) III Year (Business Studies)

1. To provide students understanding of the problems, techniques and administration of personal management and human resource development.

2. To provide knowledge of various labour laws which are applicable to business units.

3. To impart knowledge of the concepts, techniques and management of advertising.

4. To impart knowledge about the handling of industrial disputes and maintaining industrial relations.

5. To familiarise the students with the basic concepts and practices of marketing.

6. To impart knowledge of policies procedures and techniques of sales management.

B. Com. (Professional) III Year (Business Economics)

1. To impart to the students knowledge of the important aspects of foreign trade and its fInancing.

2. To impart knowledge to the students with the basic concepts and principles of commercial banks and their operations.

3. To provide knowledge to students of the main provisions of various banking laws and their application.

4. To prepare students for the professional career in the management of export procedures and policy.
5. To impart knowledge to the students of the organisation, management and functioning of co-operative banking institutions.
6. To acquaint the students with the main aspects of import policy and procedures as prevalent in India.

M.Com (Accounting)

1. To develop the understanding and skills to prepare accounts of corporate sector and also to impart knowledge in current issues in the area of accounting.
2. To acquaint the students with a coherent set of logical principles and a general frame of reference for the evaluation and development of sound accounting practices.
3. To develop an understanding of the analytical tools necessary for developing a basic framework for designing and operating a management control system.
4. To acquaint the participants with some major operations, research techniques as also the application of computer in business systems.
5. To give an exposure to various accounting issues in international business operations and corporate reporting.
6. To give an integrated view of tax laws and finance to assess and apply direct tax measures in managerial decisions.
7. To develop understanding of accounting tools and information and their use in managerial decision-making.

8. To provide understanding of direct tax laws including the rules, notifications and case law pertaining thereto and their application to different like business situations.
9. To acquaint students with the application of statistical tools in the area of business decision-making.
10. To develop an understanding of the finance function and relevant techniques of financial administration.

M. Com. (Business Studies)

1. To provide understanding of the general theory of management.
2. To provide knowledge of organisation behaviour, group dynamics and various important aspects related to industrial psychology.
3. To provide an understanding of the problems and techniques employed in the field of personnel management.
4. To impart knowledge about production techniques, process and operations management tools.
5. To provide knowledge and develop skills in the use of tools and techniques of accounting.
6. To develop an understanding of the finance function and relevant techniques of financial administration.
7. To develop understanding of the marketing functions and strategies.
8. To provide an insight into process of decision-making, policy formulation and strategic management.
9. To give an understanding of concepts, design and practice of management information system.

10. To provide understanding of the rationale, growth problems and policies of public enterprises, with special reference to India.

M. Com. (Business Economics)

1. To provide knowledge of production function, theory of firm, factor pricing and economic problems at unit level.
2. To provide understanding of the economic factors governing the operation of industry.
3. To acquaint students with the application of statistical tools in the area of business decision-making.
4. To provide understanding of the functioning of financial markets and institutions and their role in Indian economy.
5. To provide understanding of economic principles and issues at macro-level and to develop ability to analyse and apply them to current economic issues.
6. To provide understanding of international economic environment, international monetary mechanism and institutions.
7. To develop an understanding of the current industrial relations situation and the role of personnel management.
8. To provide understanding of growth models planning process and its methodology.
9. To provide an understanding to the students of the rationale, growth, problems and policies of public enterprises, with special reference to India.
10. To provide understanding of the public finance and budgetary practices in India.

Post-Graduate Diploma in Cost Accounting

1. To provide an insight into the factory management, engineering economics and production planning.
2. To make the students aware of the format and procedures and develop skills in accounting of major elements of cost.
3. To provide a working knowledge of the various methods and techniques of costing as employed in present day business enterprises for cost entertainment and cost control.
4. To provide students an insight into the dimension of the cost and management audit.

Post-Graduate Diploma in Personnel Management

1. To provide knowledge of various aspects of personnel policies, management and problems.
2. To provide knowledge of industrial relations and its impact on national economy.
3. To provide knowledge of how to develop human resources in a modern organisation so as to enhance their contribution to organisation.
4. To acquaint the students with the legal framework governing Indian labour.

Post-Graduate Diploma in Portfolio Management

1. To acquaint the students with the theory and practice of portfolio management.
2. To familiarise the students with the functioning and development of the Indian capital market.
3. To make the students conversant with the principal provisions of various enactments as they affect the investment and portfolio decisions of the investors.

4. To acquaint the students with the techniques of preparing, analysing and interpreting the annual accounts.

Post-Graduate Diploma in Entrepreneurship and Small Scale Unit Management

1. To give exposure to the students to entrepreneurship culture and industrial growth and with a view to enabling them to set-up and manage small units.
2. To acquaint the students with the concept and tools of accounting and finance and the relevant provision of taxation.
3. To provide knowledge of techniques of formulation and appraisal of viable units.
4. To acquaint the students with functional areas of management as applied to small ventures.

Post-Graduate Deploma in Foreign Trade

1. To acquaint the students with planning, techniques and organisation of international marketing and apprise them with managerial problems in this regard.
2. To impart knowledge about import and export procedures and make the students familiar with related documents.
3. To impart knowledge about international economic systems cooperation and various aspects of foreign trade in India.
4. To acquaint the students with various legal provision affecting foreign trade and also to impart knowledge of overseas marketing research.

2

Teaching Technique

Successful classroom instruction depends upon the technique of teaching; through it, the learning activity of the pupils is guided. Pupil activity, without the organisation of effort and material to achieve a definite goal, would be a waste of time and effort and would not achieve satisfactory results in content learned, or in study habits. It is the teaching technique that provides this guidance for the pupils. Therefore, the instructional period should be a learning period for the pupils. The general principles of learning should have specific application in every actual teaching situation. Whenever a teacher is teaching, the pupils should be engaged in suitable learning activities, utilising the proper study technique and developing skill in such activities. The technique of teaching should be adapted to the technique of learning, which the pupils use in their work. Since the outcomes of teaching and learning are both in pupil achievement, the technique of teaching as well as that of learning depends upon the learning outcomes being sought by the pupil at any time.

The technique of teaching must be used as a means to an end, and must be improved through research and experimentation. The technique to be used must be carefully selected and must be adjusted to the subject, to the pupils, and to the objectives. It should centre upon the primary laws of learning. The technique employed by the teacher in the classroom is of prime importance to the education of children.

The validity of any technique in teaching is measured by the extent to which it contributes to the realisation of the specific and general objectives of education.

There is a specialised learning technique for each type of learning. From psychology and education we have the following general conclusion in this respect: (1) knowledge is best gained through the technique called the question and answer; (2) skill and habits may be acquired through the drill and practice technique; (3) attitudes and appreciation may be best developed by effective use of the learning technique called appreciation.

Standards that Govern the Selection of Technique

It is generally accepted that technique is to teaching and method is to learning. The following standards must be observed by the teacher in the selection of his technique:

1. The Technique should be selected on the Basis of Its Direct Effect Upon Some Essential Phase of the Learner's Learning Performance. The technique will be as good as its good effect upon the mental processes involved in dealing with the subject-matter presented to the learner. Likewise, the effectiveness of any technique is measured by the growth experienced by the learner.

2. The Technique should be Selected According to the Nature and Maturity of the Pupils or of the Class. A certain technique may not be equally effective with all pupils in the group. The teacher must be alert to discover the reactions of the pupils and to adapt his technique to the varying characteristics of the pupils.

3. The Technique must be Selected According to the Nature of the Subject-matter. The presentation of the subject-matter requires a technique different from that which is effective in presenting formal materials in the same subject. Likewise, the technique that proves effective in dealing with history may not be suited to the presentation of language materials, and mathematics, government, physics, etc., may still require different technique to render their presentation effective. The teacher must adapt his technique to the nature and purpose of the subject-matter.

4. The Technique should be Selected on the Basis of the Ability and Training of the Teacher who would Employ it. The teacher should not attempt to practice any kind of technique that is foreign to him. He should study his own nature and know his own weakness and limitation. A phase is known to him and is easy for him to perform.

5. The Technique should be Selected According to the Time Alloted to the Subject. A short period will require a different kind of practice from that which is best adapted for a long period. If the teaching period is devoted to drill, review, or the presentation of a new lesson, the technique must be different, even though the length of time is the same.

Rules Governing the Use of Techniques

The following rules should be observed in the use of technique:

1. The Technique should be Used as a Means to an End. The teacher should never centre his attention upon his technique to the extent that his chief concern is to show off his performance. Attention should centre at all times on the learning performance of the pupils. As a rule, the more the technique of the teacher is evident the less effective it is, and *vice versa.*

3. The Technique should he Judged by the Effect it Produces Upon Each Particular Situation. However, the act that is effective at one time in one situation may not be effective at another time in another situation. The teacher should constantly adapt his technique to the securing of the desired results in each teaching situation.

3. The Technique should be Adjusted to the Physical and Mental Growth of the Pupils. Their interest should be taken into consideration. The technique which appeals most to the pupils should always be utilised.

4. The Technique should Utilise the Primary Laws of Learning Such as Readiness, Exercise, and Effect. The values of these laws are generally recognised in any method or technique of teaching.

5. The Technique should be Used According to the Nature and Aims of the Subject-matter. The technique of the teacher is oftentimes influenced by the nature and aims of the lesson.

Technique in the Use of Question-and-Answer Type of Recitation

Nature and Importance of Questioning. The question-and-answer method of teaching has been subject to as much the lame criticism as the other traditional methods. Nevertheless, this method can also be very fruitful if used intelligently. It should be employed with father stringent limitations. Nothing can be more deadly, more routine, than merely asking a series of questions of one pupil after another. To be effective, the question-and-answer method must be used with a great deal more imagination, ingenuity, and intelligence in order to yield its best results. It would be impossible to consider adequately methods of teaching without recognising the question as an essential element in all teaching procedures. The question is the key to all educative activity above the habit-skill level.

The importance of questioning has been recognised by the great teachers of method for many generations. The question-and-answer method, otherwise known as the Socratic Method, is an almost universal method of teaching, the technique of which all teachers should know. The technique is indefinitely more memorised, but upon the ability of the pupils to analyse, evaluate, and generalise in constructive fashion from the text, which is expected only as a starting point for rigorous mental activity. The teacher must keep the class moving steadily and progressively in the direction of its ultimate goal and, if possible, toward the realisation of its immediate objectives. A complete understanding of the nature of questioning and skill in its use are fundamental in all teaching procedures.

In the classroom the question assumes a still more important role. It is a key to all educative activity. In a large number of schools today, the period of pupil-activity in academically oriented subjects is a period devoted to question-and-answer. It is therefore imperative that the teacher has a clear understanding of all its aspects and its rule in stimulating, directing, guiding, and encouraging the learner. To meet the difficulties inherent in the case of the question under classroom conditions requires some personal equipment, on the part of the teacher, beyond a technical knowledge of the approved mechanics of questioning. It is necessary that the teacher has mastery of the subject-matter and is alert in his thinking. Unless the teacher has an intimate acquaintance with the content of the subject-matter and achieves rigorous habits of thought, successful questioning is not possible. The teacher must likewise, have a sense of relative value if she is to handle questions and responses to the class to the best advantage. The teacher must have the ability to frame questions skilfully. Self-confidence on the part of the teacher is essential in questioning. Until self-confidence is achieved by the teacher, clarity of thought is impossible.

Functions of Questions

Questions perform a varitey of functions. They are utilised largely, however, to perform the following:

1. To Measure the Pupil's Achievement in Knowledge, Habits, Abilities, Skills, and Attitudes. This is perhaps the most extensively involved function of questions. Likewise, question can be used to measure the pupil's understanding of the facts learned. Memorising of facts does not insure their understanding. One of the fundamental aims of education is to develop understanding or insight

2. To Challenge Individual Attention. If properly used, the question is very effective in challenging attention. Stimulating questions will arouse intense interest which is the basis of attention. The attention of an unattentive pupil may be gained back through the use of questions. In like manner, in a class growing listless, a stimulating question will sometimes arouse intense interest.

3. To Stimulate Interest in the Work at Hand. The question, to stimulate interest, must be adopted to the experience and ability of the pupil and should create a situation likely to involve a desire to know. Curiosity or interest is the best stimulus to learning that can be utilised by the teacher. Questioning is also effective as a means of securing a vital interest in the new or advance assignment. It is wise for the teacher to stimulate the pupil's thinking so that questions that lead to definite intellectual interests will arise. To stimulate interest, classroom questions should be predominantly thought-provoking in nature.

4. To Develop the Power of Evaluation. Evaluation is one phase of true thinking, though more prominent in some types of thought than in others. The teacher can by, the use of discriminating questions, lead the pupils to evaluate carefully the value of data in textbooks, both for correctness and relative significance. Pupils are constantly called upon to evaluate the merit of this fact over other facts, as the basis for intelligent generalisation.

5. To Help Pupils to Correlate Past Experiences to the New Lesson. Most pupils have read, travelled, and had other experiences that may have an important bearing upon the understanding of a given lesson. It is a wise teacher who will use the question to draw upon this valuable reservoir to supplement and interpret data already before the class. Questions related to the past experiences of the pupils are useful in teaching developmental lessons.

6. To Develop the Power of Organisation. The use of related questions will lead the pupils to see the relation of one fact to another. It is the work of the teacher to formulate questions that will lead the pupil to see the relation of one fact to another, and the possible effect of that relationship upon broader interpretation and conclusion.

7. To Develop Appreciation. A well-directed series of questions may create likes and dislikes. Subtle suggestions in the form of questions will serve this purpose. Social psychology has long recognised the potency of suggestion in the conditioning of favourable or unfavourable attitudes and the control of social behaviour. It is important for the teacher to realise that the proper question technique maybe a help in fostering such attitudes.

8. To Stimulate Thought. It is generally accepted that at the heart of every question there is a problem. At certain stages in learning for some individuals, even the most simple memory questions will evoke thought. In modern education the primary function of the question is the stimulation of thought.

Characteristics of Good Questions

Questions, to be worthwhile, must have the following characteristics:

1. They must be Carefully Planned. Questions to be asked should be prepared in advance. They should be selected with care and formulated with reference to the objective set up. Carefully planned questions are prerequisites to good teaching and effective learning. They serve as the teacher's guide for effective teaching. Careful planning is a part of any learning process.

2. They must be Brief and Direct. Questions should be brief and direct to the point of clearness. They should be made simply and reasonably short, so that their meanings can be easily grasped by the pupils. There should be no doubt in the minds of the pupils as to what the teacher means, in order that there may be the desired concentration of thought upon the answer. This makes for easy understanding, and renders the question comprehensible to pupils of varying degrees of intelligence.

3. They must be Adopted to the Ability and Experience of the Pupils. Questions should be adapted to the ability, interest, experience, and maturity of the pupils; otherwise they cannot promote profitable reflection and thinking. Only when they are so adapted can the pupils be expected to grasp the full significance of the question. They should be adapted also to the nature and aims of the lesson. Only questions involving the degree of comprehension which the individual has attained should be asked.

4. They should Stimulate Thinking and Reasoning. Questions should stimulate the thinking and reasoning power of the pupils. Thought-provoking questions will accomplish this objective and will further stimulate reflection and encourage favourable expression. Unless the lesson is of a drill type, it should contain a predominance of 'thought-provoking questions.' Direct questions should generally be avoided.' "Yes" and "No" answers do not evince thought. Single-word answers, as a rule; should be accepted only in drill work. Where thought has not been stimulated, the exercise must be considered a failure.

5. They must Allow Logical Order. For checking up a developmental lesson, the questions given should be in logical order so that the pupils may have a clear idea of the wholeness of the lesson. Otherwise, there will be confusion in the pupils' minds ill regard to the lesson. Besides, the pupil will fail to obtain an adequate conception of the teacher's purpose. This principle, however should not be observed in conducting drill or review lesson by means of questions.

6. They must be Free from the Wording of the Textbook. Questions, to be effective, must be free from the language of the textbook in order to stimulate initiative and the thinking and reasoning power of the pupils. Moreover, questions that are worded originally and apart from the textbook will require independence of thought and study on the part of the pupils. The questions in the textbooks, may, however, be used to aid in review, to direct the thought to all phases of the subject, or to awaken interest in further study or investigation. The questions in the textbook should not be used in conducting the recitation.

7. They must Follow Certain Aims. Questions should formulated according to the aim or purpose of the teacher. Memory questions should be formulated somewhat differently when the purpose is to elicit an opinion or to stimulate discussion. To the teacher, the observer, and the pupils, the questions should have direct relation to the objectives of the lesson or course. Without a specific aim, no matter how engaging the manner of the teacher, or how well he puts his questions, the desired end will not be accomplished. There must always be a clearly conceived purpose in every recitation and even in each of the questions that are put to the class. Questions that are purposeless soon kill the spirit of the class.

8. They must be Definite in Requirement. Definiteness in requirement is necessary to secure clearness. Questions which are definite in requirement are more objective, valid, and reliable. When a question is susceptible of two or more interpretations, its value is lost. The utmost care in the formulation of questions is necessary to insure that ideas are clearly conveyed from teacher to pupil.

9. They must be Related to One Another. Questions should be properly related to one another to establish a relationship between facts or points. Related questions will lead to better organisation of the points learned, for they can bridge the gap from point to point.

10. They should be of Varying Difficulty. Questions should be of varying difficulty or degree. Beginning questions should be easy enough to stimulate the interest of the pupils. As the recitation progresses, the more difficult questions should be given.

Use of Question-and-Answer Technique

Questions perform a variety of functions. The teacher should keep in mind that one function of instrumental questions is to facilitate the teaching process toward the achievement of educational aims. The use of questions as a teaching device should not be considered as being limited to testing. The other important functions of the question-and-answer procedure which should be recognised are:

1. In Drill Work. Questions are often used to strengthen the connection formed in order to make it automatic. When the questioning is for the purpose of drill, limited responses and speed in reaction are desirable. In this case the practice must recognise the laws of learning underlying the drill process. Good teachers have recognised the value of frequent drills on important facts conducted through rapid questioning.

2. In Diagnosing the Weakness of the Pupils. As a means of diagnosing, the test question is highly valuable in that it gives direction to teaching and learning. The teacher's questions help bring out the points that the pupils have overlooked.

3. In Guiding the Pupils in the Recitation. By means of questions, the teacher can guide or help the pupils is the organisation, analysis, and evaluation of the lesson. The interpretation of the reading materials may be aided by careful questioning.

4. In Furnishing Incentives to Careful Preparation. Most often, the teacher makes use of questions to create a strong desire in the pupils to do their work. Questioning is especially effective as a means of securing a vital interest in the advance assignment.

5. In Directing Attention to Certain Points. Questions can, help bring out the important points or facts in the lesson. They also can guide the pupils in their studies. The teacher can direct the attention of the class to the important points in the lesson through questions.

6. In Developing or Stimulating Thinking. Reflective thinking is best stimulated by means of questions. Classroom questions should be predominantly thought-provoking in nature. The inductive or deductive development may be utilised.

7. In Review Work. For centuries, questions have been used for review purposes. The purpose of review is to associate the old lesson with the new lesson so that the pupils may be given a view of the whole. It is the duty of the teacher to formulate questions that will lead the pupils to see the relation of one fact to another, and the possible effect of that relationship upon broader interpretation and generalisation.

8. In Verifying the Pupil's Interpretation of the Lesson Assigned. The pupil's understanding of the lesson assigned can be checked up by the use of question. Questioning can reveal to the teacher the range and breadth of the pupil's knowledge. This is perhaps the most extensively involved function of the question.

Classification of Questions

For the most part, questions should challenge thought and test the pupil's knowledge indirectly, rather than directly.

Based on this concept, questions may be classified according to their purpose or function and according to the mental process involved. There are several ways of classifying question into types. The types of question based on purpose are drill questions, factual or memory questions, developmental questions, and pivotal questions. The purpose of drill is to make mental associations automatic. Good drill questions should be short, definite, and factual. They are purely memory questions and do not demand much thinking on the part of the pupils. Memory questions require simple recall of facts. They are used in teaching content subjects. Like drill questions, memory questions do not demand much reflection. Developmental questions are often used in teaching developmental lesson. The developmental questions are useful in getting pupils to associate one detail with another so as to see their proper meaning and significance. This type of questions is often used in the teaching of history and literature. Pivotal questions are used to direct the pupil's thinking to important points. A pivotal question is a comprehensive one which goes straight to the heart of the lesson under consideration. This type is often used to help pupils to think straight and to lead him quickly to the point of difficulty. The other type of questions based on the mental process involved are the thought-provoking questions and the factual questions. Thought-provoking questions require reflective thinking before the answer can be given. The examples of thought-provoking questions are analytical, organisation, cause and effect, explanation, comparison, and imaginative questions.

Technique in Asking Questions

Technique in asking questions in any teaching situation concerns the skillful way and manner of questioning. There is no hard and fast rule governing the way questions are to be presented before the class, but there are practices that experience has shown to be ineffective. All the suggestions given in this book are subject to exception. But they are based upon the experiences of good teachers. No teacher of elementary and secondary subjects can succeed in his teaching who does not have a fair mastery of the art of questioning. The following principles are suggested:

1. Questions should not be Asked Hurriedly. They should not be given too fast nor too slowly. All questions should be asked in a slow manner and with apparent deliberation. The speed should be based on the purpose of the teacher. Only drill and review questions should be put under time pressure. Drill questions should be short and drill work brief and rapid. Such a procedure will give all the members of the class an equal opportunity to formulate tentative answers in their minds. The teacher who calls upon the pupil to answer immediately after the question is asked makes reflective thinking almost, impossible. There is little incentive to thorough and accurate thinking.

2. Questions may be Asked First Before Calling on the Pupil to Answer the Question. More pupils will thereby be stimulated to think and the recitation will not become centred upon the teacher and the pupil asked. Such a practice has the further advantage of securing general attention to class procedure and to the answer given. If the pupils know in - advance that a particular pupil is to do the answering, inattention will result. This is especially true with the traditional practice of calling on pupils by turn. If the pupils do not know when their turn is to come they will be more alert.

3. Questions should be Evenly Distributed Among the Members of the Class. As much as possible all pupils must be given an opportunity to take part in the class activities. However, in a large class, it is not always desirable that every pupil should participate each day. Each pupil should be given questions according to his need and interest. The fundamental purpose in distributing questions is to make the pupils feel that they have a share in the recitation as well as a responsibility. To accomplish this purpose, it will be well for the teacher to examine his class roll from day to day to see that he is distributing his questions accordingly.

4. Questions Once Given should not be Repeated. The practice of giving questions only once will, no doubt, make the pupils attentive during the period of questioning. Attention is challenged by not repeating the question. To repeat the question is to invite inattention. Of course, a question may be repeated when unavoidable noise at the instance of asking the question makes the hearing difficult. If a teacher makes a practice of repeating his questions, he will soon create very undesirable atmosphere of inattention which fosters careless answers. Under certain circumstances the questions may need to be repeated, but the habit of repeating questions is pedagogically unsound. Such a policy will do much to stimulate attention.

5. Questions should be Asked in a Natural and Modulated Voice. This will give the pupils opportunity to react under favourable conditions and proper stimulation. Psychologically, a quiet manner of questioning stimulates the best thinking and reveals the willingness to teach. Questioning should be natural and interesting, and the conversational tone of voice is considered the best.

6. Questions that are Quite Difficult should be Addressed to the Bright Pupils. Such a practice is a true recognition of individual differences and of the law of satisfaction. Thus the bright pupils will be given an opportunity to develop their thinking and reasoning power if the difficult questions are addressed to them. This should not be construed to mean that the slow pupils are to relax and to wait for an easy question while the brighter pupil is answering a difficult question. What the teacher should do is to formulate questions that will best challenge the ability of every member of the class and the answers to which are within the comprehension of all.

7. The Pupils should be Encouraged to ask Questions. This will give them the opportunity to clear their doubts on certain points in the lesson presented or discussed. The teacher should use every possible means to make the pupils participate in class work through questions. It is not an uncommon experience for the writer, as a supervisor, to observe teachers being embarrassed when questioned by the pupils. In a democratic country like the India, the pupils, like the teachers, have the right to ask questions. However, only questions related to the lesson should be entertained. Questions asked by the pupils are not necessarily to be answered by the teacher. It is a good practice to ask the pupils to help answer their own questions.

8. The Teacher should Show Adaptability in Questioning. It is impossible for the teacher to anticipate fully the classroom situation as it will be. Well-planned questions may need to be cast aside and new ones formulated as the classroom exigencies demand. The teacher should show such close rapport with the class and such mastery of the subject that questions will appear fresh blown for the moment, and perfectly at point. The teacher should never be afraid to venture an off hand question not stated in the lesson plan. Adaptability in questioning is essential in a democratic teaching process.

9. Inattentive or Mischievous Pupils should be Made the Targets of Questions. The main purpose is to gain their attention or to interest them in the lesson. This method is a good means of handling disciplinary situations arising from inattention. When pupils know that they are called because of inattention, they are apt to give respectful attention, especially if they failed to study their lessons. Questioning should be done to arouse interest and to stimulate the pupils into activity.

10. There should be no Regular or Systematic Order in Asking Questions. By following a systematic order in questioning, the teacher unwrittingly suggests to the pupils their turn to recite; therefore, they will be more likely to pay attention only when they are about to be called upon. Following a regular or systematic order in asking questions will make the recitation mechanical rather than rational. A pupil should be called upon for some good reason apparent in the situation and often to all or several members of the class.

11. The Teacher should Require Courtesy in Questioning. The occasional eagerness of the pupils to ask questions leads at times to several questions being propounded to the teacher simultaneously. It is a splendid opportunity for the teacher to show the class how courtesy and self-restraint often made both for speed and for the realisation of the desired objectives. Failure to insist upon one question at a time from the class inevitably leads to confusion, and later to bad disciplinary problems. It cannot be denied that some pupils are generally discourteous in their questions.

12. The Teacher should Recognise the Timeliness of the Questions Asked by the Pupils. Not all questions by the pupils should be entertained. Only questions related to the lesson under discussion should be welcomed by the teacher. Likewise, if they are significant to the class and have more educational value than the lesson itself, it is proper to consider them. The more the teacher can bring pupils to ask questions, the more certain they can be that education is taking place in the classroom. A question asked by the pupils also has an important bearing on teachersuccess

Technique in Dealing with Answers to Questions

As regards the manner of dealing with the answers given by the pupils, there is no hard and fast rule to follow. The following principles, however, are suggested:

1. Correct Answers should be Followed by an Encouraging Remark. This will stimulate the pupils to further study and better reactions. The nature of commendation should be judged by the nature of the response given and the ability of the individual concerned. The teacher should give appreciative consideration to all pupils' answers to make them feel that their contributions are worthwhile even though they may not be exactly what the teacher wants.

2. Answers Given by the Pupils should not be Repeated by the Teachers. The teacher should exercise discretion in repeating answers. An answers giving Important facts or information may be repeated for emphasis especially if such an answer is to be the source of another question. An answer may also be repeated if the sentence construction needs correction or improvement. If the answer must be repeated, have the pupil do it.

3. The Pupils should be Made to Observe Correct English Usage in Answering. The educational value of good and correct expression is beyond doubt. Modern education insists that the knowledge of correct grammatical form or correct English usage is a matter of habit formation. The teacher should require his pupils to frame their answers in good English. It is generally accepted that good English habits can only be developed through correct practice.

4. Insist on Clearness on Every Point Expressed by the Pupils. Answers which are not the result of careful thinking should not be accepted. Habits of clear thinking should be developed. This will help eliminate the necessity of repeating the pupil's answer. Many teachers make the mistake of drawing the discussion to a close too soon with an air of finality. The pupil's discussion should not be left behind in fragmentary order. With respect to the individual recitation, the pupil who has the floor should be encouraged to continue reciting until he has, if possible, made a significant contribution to the discussion.

5. Answering in Concert should be Discouraged. It should be allowed only in special or exceptional cases not regularly. Besides, answering in chorus has little diagnostic value. This manner of answering is permissible if the teacher's purpose is either to arouse the interest of the pupils or to elicit group judgement.

6. Encourage Liberal Expression of Views in Answering Questions. Answers of some length should be encouraged among our ,pupils in grades. This will train them to express themselves with ease and intelligence. The timid pupils should be encouraged to take part in the discussion. Generally, the teacher is likely to forget the timid pupil who does not volunteer to recite. The teacher should endeavour to give such a pupil special encouragement and must refrain from comments that would tend to belittle his contribution.

7. The Teacher should Never Bluff in Answering a Pupil's Question. When the teacher cannot answer questions asked by the pupils, he must frankly say so. The teacher has nothing to gain by bluffing but loss of pupil-respect. Pupils are quick to detect when a teacher bluffing his way. On the other hand, a frank admission as a matter of course that the teacher is not a medium of all wisdom will be accepted with increased respect for the teacher. However, it cannot be. denied that a teacher cannot afford to be too often put in a position where lack of essential knowledge must be admitted.

8. The Pupils should Never be Assisted in the Formulation of their Answers. Let them make their contribution unassisted. It is an accepted principle that one learns by reacting; hence, a pupil' should be trained to rely on his own resources and to frame his answer without assistance from the teacher. However, slow pupils may be helped in the formulation of their answers either by suggestions or by the use of guide questions. This practice will relieve them of the embarrassment occasioned by their slow thinking. Under ordinary circumstances, however, pupils should rely upon their own resources in answering questions.

Technique in Conducting Recitation

There is no one procedure or technique that can be used for the conduct of the recitation. Rather, the plan adopted must vary with the subject and with the aims of the teacher and the pupils. The teacher must bear in mind that practically very method used in the classroom will involve elements of the lecture of the recitation. It is therefore, necessary to recognise the flexible nature of the recitation and the manner of its use. There are certain suggestions on the technique of conducting the recitation with merit and consideration. A good technique in conducting the recitation involes a number of principles such as the following:

1. Recitation should be Carefully Planned. A good recitation program should be well planned if it would carry out the purpose of the teaching period. Any well-planned activity produces a good effect. The plan must be based on the modem concept of the recitation. The basic elements of planning as applied to teaching and learning must be well considered by the teacher. The plan must be centred on the growth of each individual.

2. Recitation should be Well Organised to Promote Unity of Thought. A good teaching technique is one that is systematic and well organised. A well-organised recitation will give the pupils a clear picture of the wholeness of the lesson rather than its disconnectedness in units of facts.

3. Recitation should Provide for Pupil Activity and Expression. Class activities such as debates, dramatics, and discussion should be made a regular part of the recitation. Creative expression can come only when provision is made for a wide range of response and when differentiation of response is encouraged by the teacher.

4. Recitation should be so Regulated as to Meet Individual Differences. A good recitation technique respects those differences and makes provision for a procedure that will suit individual characteristics. Attention to individual differences is an important factor in teaching.

5. Recitation should be Well Motivated. A carefully introduced recitation establishes a favourable attitude toward the work and provides a proper setting for the new lesson. An attitude of alert eagerness on the part of the teacher is likely to arouse a similar attitude in the class.

6. Recitation should be Adopted to the Aim and Purpose of the Teacher. How the recitation should be conducted depends upon the purpose of the teacher and the aim of the lesson. Learning is effective when it is purposeful.

7. Recitation should Utilise the Appropriate Lesson Type. The purpose rather than the method determines the type to be used. The type should be selected with reference to the aim, subject, grade, and the maturity of the pupils.

8. Recitation should Provide Review Work for the Pupils. This will give the pupils an opportunity to master the subject-matter previously learned. It will also give the teacher an opportunity to diagnose the weakness of his pupils and to discover their readiness for the next lesson.

9. Recitation should Provide Pupil's Cooperation in the Planning. This can be done without abdication of the prerogatives of the teacher to use his mature judgement in the planning of the lesson. The degree to which the teacher may permit or encourage participation in planning depends upon the ability and experience of the pupils. It is through the pupil's participation that the most legitimate forms of cooperation may be sought.

10. Recitation should Stimulate the Thinking and Reasoning Power of the Pupils. A good recitation technique allows for reflective thinking and provides opportunity for spontaneous expression.

Poor Recitation Technique

A poor recitation is often due to wrong technique such as the following :

1. Allowing the Recitation to Become a Dull Narration of the Lesson Assigned. Some teachers are contented with merely being able to hear by themselves the pupil reciting. The pupil should address the class and not the teacher.

2. Allowing the Pupils to Sit Lazily While Reciting. This is one of the causes of poor classroom management. Pupils should be stimulated in order that they may become active mentally and physically.

3. Failure of Correct Errors in English During the Recitation. Errors made by the pupils should be corrected in order to develop the desired language habits. The pupils should be encouraged to correct their own errors in English; it should not always be the teacher who should do it.

4. Interrupting Pupils who are Reciting. It is bad technique to interrupt a pupil in the midst of his talk. The teacher should not stop the pupil just to criticise him.

5. The Teacher Reciting for the Pupils. The teacher should not answer his own questions nor complete the answers of the pupils. There should be more activity on the part of the pupils and less on the part of the teacher.

6. Confining the Recitation to a Few Pupils. Most often the recitation is dominated by the bright pupils. The majority of the pupils are neglected. The questions should be properly distributed.

Technique in Conducting Socialised Type of Recitation

The socialised recitation may be either formal or informal. The socialised recitation is that form of recitation in which the members of the class take turns in presiding over and in conducting the recitation. There are certain suggestions regarding the technique of conducting the formal or informal socialised types of recitation. The following principles are suggested:

1. The Teacher should Repress his own Tendency to Monopolise the Discussion. The pupils should be given more opportunity to participate in the discussion. The theory of self-activity should be foremost in the mind of the teacher.

2. The Teacher should Encourage the Members of the Class not to Limit their Discussion to the Textbooks Alone. Other sources should be utilised to stimulate the interest of the class.

3. The Teacher should Train the Leader in the Proper Procedure. The integrity of the group must be preserved. Fairness and courtesy must be observed by the leader and the members of the class.

4. The Teacher should Encourage the Members of the Class to Address Themselves to the Group. The whole responsibility should be made to rest on the leader or group rather than on the teacher. This is one of the characteristics of a socialised class.

Techniques in the Use of Visual Devices

The alternative for pure abstraction in learning and teaching appears to be such concrete materials or illustrations as the pupils may see, feel, and manipulate. Most schools could not afford to provide a concrete basis for all educational activity, even though it were possible or desirable. In teaching and in learning, visual devices supply one form of aid to attention, understanding, imagination, and incentive to action. Visual devices are used to attract attention. The teacher who has a repertoire of good visual devices at hand usually maintains full class attention. Visual devices are also used to facilitate reasoning and understanding. The fundamental reason for the use of visual aids is to aid reasoning and understanding. Visual devices are further used to stimulate imagination and provide incentives to action. The teacher must use the power of word symbolism and concrete materials to fire the imagination, arouse the emotions, and incite to actions. Unfortunately, teachers have seriously cramped the larger possibilities of intellectual development of the pupils through the failure to adequate stimulation of the imagination and the will to intellectual activity.

To make use of visual devices most effectively, certain prerequisites must be observed. The technique in the presentation of visual aids varies somewhat with each of their type. The standard suggested does not apply with equal force in every situation. The following principles are related to the use of visual devices:

1. Use of Visual Aids should be Well Planned by the Teacher. The teacher needs to have all visual aids properly classified and ready for instant use. When a number of materials are to be used, they should be arranged in order so that each will be used in proper turn. Where mechanisms are involved; they should be carefully checked to insure their perfect working condition before use. No detail that would detract from the effective use of the visual aids should be overlooked. Visual aids should be viewed in their relation to good teaching.

2. Use of Any Type of Visual Aids should be for Some Definite Teaching Purpose. The temptation to use visual devices in a vague assurance that they will be helpful too often accomplishes nothing. Visual aids should be for some definite teaching purpose or for, a definite function to perform. They are not to be used just to attract attention in a general way. They should serve a specific purpose in the development of the lesson. The teacher should see clearly a real need for visual aids, and then select a concrete material that will actually assist the pupils to overcome their difficulties.

3. Visual Aids should be Used Judiciously by the Teacher. It cannot be denied that too many devices used may confuse, rather than enlighten. One writer warns against too many devices; another insists that danger lies in the use of too few. Judged in the light of extended observation, the danger would seem to lie in under, rather than over use. The greatest danger lies in a profuse use of concrete materials in and out of the season without due regard to actual needs. The number of devices and the extent to which they should be given, must remain a matter of discretion on the part of the teacher.

4. Visual Aids should be Used to Furnish Illustrations, During the Course of the Lecture or Development of the Lesson. The important function of illustrations is to facilitate understanding of the lesson presented or developed. Most pupils can think better if they tie their thinking to some definite concrete material observed. In addition, they insure more effective learning and more permanent retention than does lecture alone.

5. Visual Aids should be Used to Supply Adequate Imagery in Some Particular Subjects. For example, in the study of plants and industries, such visual aids as pictures, films, slides, and graphs are rich sources of imagery for the pupils. Vivid and realistic imagery should be evoked with care.

6. Visual Aids should be Used Only When the Lesson Presented does not Furnish a Basis for Appreciation. The approach to a new lesson or subject may be made more attractive and more interesting by the use of concrete materials. Through the use of visual aids it is possible to arouse interest in learning. The teacher can, likewise, maintain full Class attention through the use of visual aids.

7. Use Sparingly Devices or Illustrations of Personal Experiences-type. It cannot be denied that one's personal experiences is most vivid and replete in mental imagery. It is most natural that recall should bring to the free appropriate experiences to fit a given situation. The danger lies in the impression of egotism that may be left as an unwholesome after-effect.

8. The Use of Visual Aids by the Pupils should be Encouraged to Give Vitality to their Recitations and Reports. Visual aids such as models, diagrams, pictures, and demonstrations add to the value of the recitation. They are valuable in clarifying the thinking and in perfecting the understanding of the pupils. Abstract ideas are also made concrete in the minds of the students through the use of visual aids.

9. Visual Aids should be Used in Summarising a Given Unit or Phase of Work. Pictures, objects, slides, and films have given good results as teaching devices. Outlines, graphs, diagrams, and charts are also effective aids to summarisation. Visual aids make it easier to concentrate on the materials learned or to see their relationship. The wholeness of the lesson learned can be illustrated through the use of visual aids.

10. The Blackboard should be Used by the Pupil to Diagram or to Illustrate his Ideas if Such a Procedure would Contribute to the Effectiveness of his Discourses or Explanation. The blackboard is one of the most; useful devices available as a visual aid in teaching and in learning. It is also used to challenge the pupil's attention.

11. Varied Types of Visual Devices should be Used. It is an accepted fact that a variety of visual aids reduces monotony to a minimum. Pupils should be encouraged to collect illustrative materials from home magazines and other publications. This can be done during an activity period. Different types of learning call for different types of visual devices.

12. The Teacher must See to it that Visual Aids are Visible to All. The danger in the use of visual devices is that they are not made sufficiently visible to all pupils to be of value. The teachers who use small pictures with light colours, or small models, are likely to err in this respect. To be of value to the pupils, visual aids must be big or bright enough in order to be visible to all.

Technique in Developing Appreciation

It is generally maintained that education should also aim to develop the power of appreciation and enjoyment. Appreciation may be defined as sympathetic understanding, or understanding coupled with a feeling of pleasure or satisfaction. A well developed appreciation is exemplified in the appreciation of good books and magazines. The development of the power of appreciation constitutes a tremendous educational responsibility on all school levels. The encouragement of an appreciative attitude in learning is a recognised function of education. No less important in the educational program of any organised school system is the education of the emotions.

Appreciation belongs to the general field of feeling rather than of knowing. However, appreciation involves an intellectual state, the addition of which makes the total complex mote of an emotional rather than of a cognitive nature. It may grow out of an active attitude or emotion. Appreciation always involves emotional tone, otherwise it could not be enjoyed.

If we want the rising generation to care for good pictures, music, and literature; to dislike the ugly, the unclean, the untidy, and the unfitting; and to raise the standards of living, we must definitely include training for these ends in our school plans and procedures. It may be urged that all these ends are accomplished by the lesson which impart information in regard to the various phases of knowledge, but knowledge does not always include the feeling of appreciation which affects ideals.

Types of Appreciation

Appreciation is of four different types which are of utmost importance to the teacher. They are: (1) appreciation of the beautiful, (2) appreciation of human nature, (3) appreciation of the humorous, and (4) appreciation of the intellectual powers.

1. Appreciation of Beauty is Usually Discussed Under the Head of Aesthetic Emotions. Most writers agree that the stimulus for aesthetic appreciation must be a sense percept, or an image of some sensed objects. Nature, arts, music, literature, and the dance are chief source of aesthetic appreciation. This type of appreciation involves emotional pleasures and reactions caused by the beauty of the things. Since good taste, beauty, and other aesthetic elements are found in many forms, appreciation has many objects upon which it may be exercised. Appreciation may be aroused in any environment, and by the work of either man or nature. Our great need is to learn to open our eyes and see the possibilities for aesthetic appreciation all about us.

2. Appreciation of Human Nature Denotes the Appreciation of the Value of Human Life—Appreciation of Great Characters, and so on. Some writers classify this type of appreciation under moral feelings. These feelings are stimulated by such studies as literature and social science subjects which deal with human life. In geography, history, and economics, we ought not to fail to cultivate it on the basis of lofty motives, hardship overcome, and suffering nobly borne. It is a valuable part of education to arouse appreciation for the spirit and labor of human beings. This appreciation has its source in the social instincts, but it must be developed and trained.

3. Appreciation of Intellectual Powers Refers to the Enjoyment of a Piece of Literature. Appreciation of the meaning expressed is the thing that can arouse feeling. This type of appreciation often results from the individuals desire to know and to experience the feeling of satisfaction. In brief, intellectual appreciation is an attitude or feeling towards questions of truth.

4. Appreciation of Humour has Many of the Characteristics of the First Two Types of Appreciation Mentioned Above. Webster defines humour as "appreciation of ludicrous or absurdly incongrous elements in ideas, situations, happenings, or acts." This type of appreciation may be exercised by reading comics in books, magazines, and newspapers which deal with human life. Humour adds to good mental health to be able to see the light side of the darkest corner.

Principles in Developing Appreciation

In developing appreciation of all kinds the following techniques or principles are suggested:

1. The Teacher must Make an Intensive and Thorough Preliminary Preparation. Everything that has to do with the subject selected must be mastered. Even the life and thoughts of the artist must be studied as intensively as possible.

2. The Teacher must Make Knowledge the Basis of Appreciation. Studies have revealed that knowledge increases appreciation. It is quite impossible to appreciate a thing fully without knowing something about its nature, characteristics, etc. The teacher should bear in mind, that the greater the intellectual basis for understanding, the greater are the possibilities for appreciation. Without understanding, we may have no sentiment, we may have the wrong sentiment, or we may be led into unwise action.

3. The Teacher himself must Appreciate What he is Teaching. It is quite difficult to teach an appreciation lesson if the teacher does not appreciate what he is teaching. Since emotional states are communicable and are frequently aroused in pupils through their imitation of the teacher, the teacher should keep his own emotional states alive. His enjoyment of literature, music, and art, his attitude toward historical situations, his approval of moral qualities, are quite likely to be reflected in his classes. In teaching for appreciation, therefore, the teacher must draw much upon himself in transmitting to the pupils the essence of his experience.

4. The Teacher should Judge the Success of his Work by the Interest he can Arouse in the Class. The class that is truly appreciative will be alert and interested. Enthusiasm is the final test of a well-taught appreciation lesson.

5. The Teacher should Direct the Emotion and Interest Aroused into Channels of Purposeful Activity. Literary clubs, social service clubs, musical clubs, art leagues, and many other similar organisations represent the crystalisation of sentiment into organised activity. The fundamental thing is to turn the sentiment into wholesome action and not to let it go to vaste.

6. The Teacher should Set-up a Definite Standard of Appreciation to be Followed or Achieved. For this reason, appreciation lessons should be taught incidentally and should be presented through many avenues. The pupils should not be forced to give expression to the feeling stimulated. A very important fact to remember is that the aesthetic appreciation is sometimes slow in its development and it is not equally distributed.

7. The Teacher must Make Use of Motivation in Developing Appreciation. The teacher's opening remarks should develop in the pupils a mind-set, a directed interest, which will give rise to a powerful impression through the thrills and climax to follow. Giving a short sketch of the author's life illustrates the application of this principle. Motivation creates an interest in the lesson and a desire for it.

8. The Teacher should Use Both Direct and Indirect Methods in Teaching. The fundamental objective in teaching appreciation is the development of interests, attitudes, and ideals, which include the recognition of values within desirable social patterns and the emotionalising of the acceptance of these social values by the pupil. The teacher should guide the pupils to a rational discovery of those attitudes, interest, and ideals worthy of emulation by direct teaching. Such teaching involves strong emphasis upon the intellectual elements without neglecting the emotional reactions that should accompany the development of interests, attitudes, and ideals. The direct teaching of the defects or evils of the dictatorship form of government preceding the Second World War is a case in point where both the, intellectual and emotional aspects of the situation were stressed with telling effect.

9. The Teacher should See to it that the Appreciation Lesson is Adapted to the Age and Experience of the Pupils. It is necessary for the teacher to be on guard against attempts to develop appreciation upon an insufficient background of experience. The teacher should also take into account the varying degrees of development of the aesthetic sense or interest of the pupils. The difference in the parents' education and interests, in other words, the difference in home environment, and similar factors enter into the situation.

●●

3

Requirement for Commerce Teacher

The teacher of commerce is expected to possess certain qualities and characteristics. Such qualities are described in brief in this chapter.

For any improvement in commerce education a well qualified and trained commerce teacher is a must. The most important of the several qualities expected of a commerce teacher is the he should be devoted to the profession of teacher. It has been observed that persons generally after taking training in commerce teaching profession switch-over to some other profession. The subject of commerce has now received wide recognition and acceptability, second only to science subjects. Therefore, it has become essential that profession of commerce teacher is taken up very seriously.

In a nut shell it can be said, "The teacher of commerce must be properly qualified person and should possess the training qualifications to teach."

Since the first and foremost duty of a commerce teacher is to teach so it is desirable that he fulfils the requirements of the profession and possesses the necessary qualifications.

Qualifications of a Commerce Teacher

A teacher of Commerce should have:

(i) A master's degree in commerce.

(ii) A bachelor's degree in education.

(iii) A good academic back-ground in Economics.

(iv) Specialisation in Commerce education.

(v) Proficiency in skill subjects.

(vi) A thorough understanding and knowledge of theories of skills.

Besides these, he should have special aptitude and training in the audio-visual aids and vocational guidance. He should have enough of professional experience and training to undertake the teaching of type-writing and short-hand efficiently. The success and prospect of vocationalisation at secondary stage largely depends upon this aspect of specialisation on the part of the commerce teacher.

Specially on instructor or a teacher. Who is required to teach short-hand and type-writing must have specialisation in these subjects and a good back-ground in teaching methods of commerce subjects. Knowledge of teaching short-hand and type-writing in English or any other regional language should be essential for a commerce teacher. Teachers for teaching short-hand and type-writing should be professional rather than M. Com. with specialisation in short-hand and typewriting. It is better to appoint a person, to teach short-hand and typewriting, who has practiced these subjects as stenographers at more than 100 words per minute for more than five years. These persons will fare well and try to develop the vocational skills of students.

Qualities of a Commerce Teacher

Various qualities which are desirable in a commerce teacher are as follows:

Personal Qualities

(i) He should have a good personality.

(ii) He should be graciously dressed.

(iii) He should be man with qualities of integrity, fairness and moral fitness.

(iv) He should possess a good physical and mental health.

(v) He should have a pleasant speaking voice.

(vi) He should be socially acceptable to his colleagues.

(vii) He should have interest and aptitude in teaching profession. In this respect Mudaliar Commission observed, "Teachers must develop a new orientation towards their work. They should look upon their work as a great social and intellectual adventure".

(viii) His relationship with his students be polite, submissive and friendly.

(ix) He must have an urge of learning new trends in this subject of Specialisation.

(x) He should be trained in use of various instructional techniques such as committee of work, question-answer, demonstration, project, discussion etc.

(xi) He should be able to function efficiently in the guidance programme of the school.

(xii) He should be able contrive and use a variety of teaching-learning procedures.

(xiii) He should be able to function well in organisation and supervision of co-curricular activities.

(xiv) He should be competent to develop, construct and use a wide variety of teaching aids.

(xv) He should be able to use variety of methods to evaluate pupils progress and his own growth as teacher.

(xvi) He should have a good understanding of current world conditions and problems.

(xvii) A good habit of study and research in commerce education.

(xviii) He should have a good understanding of the needs of students in relation to knowledge.

(xix) He should have a good proficiency of observation and records of behaviors, interest and development of students.

Interests of Commerce Teacher

A commerce teacher to be successful should have a variety of interest. These may be summarised as under:

Community Interests

(i) He must be an active member of parent-teacher association.

(ii) He should be actively interested in community activities.

(iii) He should be interested in student's clubs and other school activities.

Professional Interest

(i) He should have a knowledge of equipments of business and industry.

(ii) He must remain in touch with the latest researches in his filed of interest.

(iii) He should have a personal library of books and magazines of Commerce, Economics and Education.

(iv) He should make it a point to participate in summer schools, work-shops, refresher courses and other in-service education programmes organised for commerce teachers.

(v) He should try to acquire professional growth through higher education in Commerce, Economics and Education.

(vi) He should contribute articles to magazines of Commerce, Education, and Economics.

Training of a Commerce Teacher

In the present educational set up the commerce teacher has to be resourceful and fully equipped with all necessary informations which can help them in training students properly. To equip himself with desirable qualities a commerce teacher is expected to pass through the following phases of training programme.

(1) University Education in Commerce Subjects. M. Com. degree is a must but it would be desirable if the teacher specialises in any one or two of the commerce subjects. For becoming a teacher in short-hand and type-writing. Certain degree of efficiency must be acquired in these subjects from professional institutes or other institutes teaching and training in the art of teaching the skill. Before appointment of commerce teachers, his specialisation and degree of efficiency, he has acquired, should be taken into consideration. Thus we can say that a person being appointed as commerce teacher should be M.Com., should have office experience or practical business experience or the stenography experience of taking dictation at a high speed.

(2) Office Experience or Practical Business Experience. For becoming a successful teacher it is desirable for the would be teacher, to have some experiences of handling office procedures and situations in business. This type of experiences provide him with the confidence that is so essential to become a successful teacher. Actual experience in handling accounts book, labour saving appliances, office practice and correspondence, banking-work, import and export documents, activities concerning sale and purchase of goods etc. will help the commerce teacher to equip himself with the necessary skills and technical know-how of the various commerce programmes. These experiences will provide the commerce teachers with the necessary reliable materials required by the commerce teacher. Only theoretical knowledge is not enough for a commerce teacher to farewell in his profession and in the absence of office experience or business experience or vocational skills he is likely to cut sorry figure in his class.

(3) Teacher Training Course. After completing his formal education in university the prospective commerce teacher should be given a course of teachers training. During this course he should be imparted training in various teaching techniques. Educational psychology, History of education etc.

Teachers training in the field of Commerce started in India only in 1963-64 when such a course was offered by four regional colleges of Education. Prior to this the following provisions were made for training of commerce teachers:

(i) Training in methods of teaching elements of commerce and book-keeping in C.I.E., New Delhi, and also in secondary training college Mumbai.

(ii) In some states, short-hand courses were held for training teachers who were already in service.

(iii) Some Seminars and courses were organised by Ministry of Education Government of India during the period 1998-2000.

(4) In-Service Training. Since the persons, who became commerce teachers prior to 1965, did not receive any specialised training in commerce methodology they were not familiar with the modem methods of teaching of commerce subjects so it was essential to arrange in-service training courses for such persons.

Teachers already in service should acquire some technical knowhow of the latest methods of teaching, new educational trends and researches made in the field of commerce. He should try to develop and use some audio-visual aids, film slides etc. and should also try to maintain a profile of papers and documents used in business transactions.

Commerce teachers should try to attend seminars, training courses and work-shops organised by Regional Colleges of Education and other training colleges that have now specialised in commerce pedagogy. They should also try to keep themselves in touch with latest publication on educational philosophy and methodology of teaching and try to keep themselves abreast of latest innovations brought about in the field of education.

Commerce teachers should make it a habit to study latest journals, magazines, periodicals etc. concerning commerce subjects and allied subjects.

All these will help a commerce teacher to become a successful commerce teacher.

Phases of Training of a Commerce Teacher

1. University education in Commerce subjects.
2. Office experience or practical business.

3. Training course in Teaching Commerce subjects.
4. In-service training.

(1) University Education in Commerce Subjects. A person being appointed as commerce teacher should be M.Com., should have office experience or practical business experience or the stenography experience of taking dictation at a high speed. It would be desirable if he spccialises in anyone or two of the commerce subjects such as short-hand and type-writing. Certain degree of efficiency must be acquired in these subjects from professional institutes or other institutes teaching and training in the art of teaching the skill. His specialisation and degree of efficiency, he has acquired should be taken into consideration before appointment of commerce teacher.

2. Office Experience or Practical Business Experience. Only theoretical knowledge is not enough for a commerce teacher to farewell in his profession. In the absence of office experience or business experience or vocational skills he is likely to cut sorry figure in his class.

For becoming a successful teacher it is desirable for the would be teacher to have some experiences of handling office procedures and situations in business. This will provide him with the confidence so essential to become a successful teacher. Actual experience in handling accounts book, labour saving appliances, office practice and correspondence, banking-work, import and export documents, activities concerning sale and purchase of goods etc. will help the commerce teacher to equip himself with the necessary skills and technical know-how of the various commerce programmes. These experiences will provide him the necessary reliable materials.

Thus, a proper training should be organised, for commerce graduate/post graduate in universities followed by a minimum of six months practical training or actual experience in service in a business firm or an office before the award of degree to them.

3. Teacher Training Course. After completing his formal education in university the prospective commerce teacher should be given a course of teachers training in various teaching techniques, Educational psychology, History of education etc.

Teachers training in the field of Commerce started in India in 1963-64 by four regional colleges of Education. Prior to this the following provisions existed for training of commerce teachers:

(i) Training in methods of teaching elements of commerce and book-keeping in C.I.E., New Delhi, and also in secondary training college Mumbai.

(ii) Seminars and courses organised by Ministry of Education Government of India during the period 1958-1960 to till date.

(iii) Short-hand courses held for training teachers who were already in service in some states.

4. In-Service Training. The commerce teachers prior to 1965, did not receive any speeialised training in commerce methodology. They were not familiar with the modern methods of teaching of commerce subjects. Hence, it was thought essential to arrange in-service training courses.

Teachers already in service should acquire some technical know-how of the latest methods of teaching, new educational trends and researches made in the field of commerce. They should develop and use some audio-visual aids, film slides etc. They should maintain a profile of papers and documents used in business transactions.

They should attend seminars, training courses and workshops organised by Regional Colleges of Education and other training college. They should also keep themselves in touch with latest publication on educational philosophy and methodology of teaching and keep abreast of latest innovations brought about in the field of education.

They should study latest journals, magazines, periodicals etc. concerning commerce subjects and allied subjects.

Duties of A Commerce Teacher

In addition to teaching, the primary duty of a commerce teacher, he has to carry out following other duties in the school:

1. Maintaining discipline in the class.
2. Keeping in touch with the business community.
3. Acting as a guide to students and help them in the choice of their subjects.
4. Evaluating the students.
5. Maintaining a proper record of the progress of each student.
6. Preparing the lesson-plan.
7. Providing guidance and counselling services.
8. Preparing written reports.
9. Preparing requisition for supplies.
10. Organising co-curricular activities.
11. Taking care of the equipment.

For carrying out these duties efficiently working teachers should improve upon their knowledge, skill etc. and keep it up-to-date.

Ways of Professional Growth

1. Mastery on the Subject. Without a mastery on his subject a teacher cannot command a good respect among students.

2. Teachers Training. Only trained teachers should be appointed in schools. A course in teachers training makes him a perfect teacher. He should be well-versed in the learning process. A trained teacher will be able to look after the sociological and philosophical concepts that he is required to deal while dealing with students.

3. Professional Attitude. A teacher should be sincere to his duties and profession and possess a professional attitude towards his job.

4. Keeping Abreast of Changes. A teacher is a nation builder and to carry out his job in right earnest he should have an over-view of the present and peep into the future. He should make modifications in the patterns of education. For all these he should keep himself abreast of the changes.

5. Dynamic in Thought and Action. The best teacher tries to equip himself with the latest know-how and information required in his area of specialisation. He should continuously keep himself engaged in learning new things. Thus, he can serve better and do more justice to his profession.

6. Store of Knowledge. The teacher should have a personal library. He should collect various types of books.

7. Attending Seminar and Conferences. A good teacher should always be on the look out for an opportunity to participate in a seminar or a conference. By this participation he broadens his out-look and expands his knowledge.

8. Contribution to Paper and Journal. Good teachers contribute their mite by communicating their ideas in black and white. They publish papers in journals of repute. In this way, they help others to benefit from his their ideas.

9. Organisation of Exhibitions and Fairs. In exhibitions and fairs a teacher contributes his best ideas and students' community gets the maximum benefit. By participating in these exhibitions and fairs the students get practical experience of most of the things they have understood. Organisation of exhibitions and fairs helps in enhancing the knowledge and skill of the teacher as also of the students. Therefore, it is desirable to organise such an activity once a year.

10. Setting up of Association. Teachers' associations are set-up to make their bargaining capacity stronger. Teachers can also discuss and solve their difficult problems during meetings of such associations. Thus, an association easily becomes a forum for discussions and publications of professional articles. Teachers are likely to enrich their experiences through this association.

11. Practice Oriented. Education should be practice-oriented. Both teachers and students should maintain a profile of business, trade, industry and school. The syllabus should be modified to cater to the business needs. Emphasis should be laid of such courses in commerce for which ready market exists.

●●

4

Curriculum in Commerce

If instructions in commerce is to be worthwhile, it must be planned with the idea of achieving certain aims which represent values attained from its study. Selection of material should be made with a purpose that is to be served by commerce in the general scheme of education. In recent times we find significant changes in man's outlook on life.

It is also essential here to clearly distinguish between 'course of study' and 'curriculum'. These two terms are used synonymously but they have different meanings.

'Curriculum' represents the subjects taught in department of school and 'course of study' represents the various topics which are prescribed for teaching. Thus the 'course of study' is a selection of topics for a particular subject where as 'curriculum' is the series of subjects in the curriculum of a stream.

The 'course of study' is a statement of objectives and outlines of the course content, *e.g.* there may be a vocational commerce curriculum meant for training the students for certain vocational careers.

Need for Curriculum

The word 'curriculum' is derived from the Latin word 'curresre' which means to run. So 'curriculum' is a course or path which one runs to reach a goal. Thus curriculum includes the subject matter and all learning experiences arranged by the school for a particular subject.

The needs of life go on changing, so is education, hence we can not go on with a static curriculum. The content has to be selected according to the changing needs of society in general and the subject in particular. The curriculum has to be planned and organised in a scientific manner keeping in view the psychological requirements of the students. If the curriculum is properly organised, it enables the students to know the subject matter which they have to study. On the other hand it also makes clear to teacher, the material that they h.ave to teach to the students. It also provides the same facility to the examiner.

Construction of the Curriculum

Following principles of curriculum construction were recommended by the Secondary Education Commission (1952-53):

(i) The curriculum should be clearly understood. It specifies not only the traditional subjects taught in school but it includes the totality of experiences that peoples receive through the manifold activities that go on in the school, in the class room, library, laboratory, work shop, play grounds and in numerous informal contacts between teacher and the student. Thus the whole life of the school becomes curriculum that can touch the life of the students at all points and help in evolution of balanced personality.

(ii) The curriculum should be vitally and organically related to community life, interpreting for the child, its salient and significant features and permitting him to come in contact with some of its important activities. (activity curriculum).

(iii) Curriculum should have flexibility and variety so that it can be easily adopted for different needs and interests. It will help to keeping away a sense of frustration that generally creeps in the child if any attempt is made to teach him uncongenial subjects.

(iv) The curriculum should be such as to help to train the students not only for work but also for leisure.

(v) It should be framed in such a way that there exist as much of inter-relationship between different subjects and also between different topics in the same subject. It means that an attempt be made to keep the contents as "broad field" units so that it is easy to correlate than with life rather than narrow items of information.

Activity Centred Curriculum

Since most of the commerce subjects are vocation based so the activity curriculum is quite suitable for commerce. In the words of Rousseau, "Instead of making the child stick to his books keep him busy in workshop where his hands will work to the profit of his mind". Thus learning by doing 'by activity and experience is the first and the most natured form of learning. This has laid the foundation of activity curriculum. It is with this in mind that it was stated in Wardha Scheme of Education, "We have attempted to draft an activity curriculum which implies that our schools must be places of work experimentation and discovery and not of passive absorption imparted as second hand".

As activity curriculum generally is based on project method or problem solving method of teaching. This is quite significant in such areas as those of physical education, science, geography, history, mathematics etc. Various psychological needs of the child are satisfied to a large extent in an activity curriculum. Here we list some of the merits of activity curriculum:

(i) It helps to make the child interested in the process of learning.

(ii) It provides enough scope to the child to learn the things at his own speed.

(iii) It provides the child various opportunities of working in a group.

(iv) It is need oriented.

(v) It helps in development of a sound body.

(vi) It helps to promote a democratic spirit in the child.

(vii) It help to create a self-confidence in the child.

(viii) It gives a totality of experiences to the pupil.

(ix) It helps the child in making full utilisation of his leisure time.

(x) It helps to develop a school-community relationship.

Though there are many a merits of the activity curriculum yet it also has certain limitation. Some of the limitations of activity curriculum are as follows:

(i) It some times leads to fatigue and boredom.

(ii) In groups, it becomes difficult to achieve the aim. Sometimes misunderstanding may lead to jealousy among the participants. In such cases it becomes the duty of the teacher to coordinate the activity and remove the misunderstanding.

(iii) In the activity curriculum there is always a possibility that the participant may not be able to master any thing those he knows something about various parts of the activity.

(iv) Some times an activity may not suit all the members of a group and this leads to lack of interest in some students.

Syllabus in Commerce

Before the Secondary Education Commission Report, the course content failed to keep pace with the changes in the social, political, economic, and industrial conditions. It could not keep pace with the latest developments in Education. Theory and practice courses were bookish and theoretical, they encouraged cramming. The instructions becomes lifeless and monotonous. This has been reflected in the following observations of Mudaliar Commission:

(i) The existing curriculum is narrowly conceived.

(ii) It is bookish and theoretical.

(iii) It is the provision for practical work is not adequate.

(iv) It is over-crowded and the content is not rich and significant.

(v) It is not in accordance with the needs and capacities of adolescents.

(vi) It is examination dominated.

(vii) It does not include technical and vocational subjects, which are so essential for industrial and economic development of the country.

The importance of inclusion of technical and vocational subjects was also emphasised in its report by Sapru Committee.

A thorough revision and diversification was undertaken on the basis of recommendations made by Mudaliar Commission.

Commerce Education being so closely related with our life its curriculum has to be the nucleus of all the activities. It should, therefore, include various subjects. At the middle level the following subjects be included:

(i) Languages, *(ii)* Social Studies, *(iii)* General Science, *(iv)* Mathematics, *(v)* Arts and Music, and *(vi)* Craft and Physical Education.

At the secondary level there should be a few subjects to be taught as core subjects to be offered by all the students, the subjects to be included as core subjects be as follows:

(i) Languages, *(ii)* Social Studies, *(iii)* General Science, and *(iv)* Craft.

For commerce education a separate stream be provided at higher secondary stage and the following subjects be included for being taught in this stream:

(i) Book-keeping and Accountancy,

(ii) Elements of Commerce or Business Methods and Machinery,

(iii) Economics,

(iv) Business Correspondence,

(v) Commercial Arithmetic,

(vi) Type writing,

(vii) Short-hand,

(viii Banking, and

(ix) Work-experience etc.

Most of these subjects have been included in their syllabus majority of Boards of Education of various states in India. In certain states the courses provide option to select there or four of these subjects *e.g.* as in Maharastra which has been appreciated by Educationists. However, if this sort of freedom has to be given to the students then the schools should be fully equipped and staffed with the right type of teachers.

Though all the subjects listed above are important for commerce education but four subjects namely type writing, short-hand, book-keeping and general principles of commerce are basic to commerce and a knowledge of these subjects be imparted to all.

For "The persons joining specialised professions such as those of doctors, lawyers architects etc. The commerce education be imported on the basis of utility".

It is thus desirable that the course content in commerce programmes is broadly classified into two categories as under:

(i) Vocational Commerce Education, and

(ii) General Commerce Education.

Under the vocational commerce education the knowledge of following subjects be imparted:

(i) Stenography and Secterial practice,

(ii) Book-keeping and accounts,

(iii) Clerical and general office work, and

(iv) Office practices.

The course content for general commerce education should include the following:

(i) Consumer information-guidance,

(ii) Business administration and management,

(iii) Economics, and

(iv) Commercial geography etc.

The content and organisation of commerce course is expected to fulfil the following imperative needs if the students:

(i) It is capable of developing saleable skills amongst the pupils.

(ii) It develops in the student a clear understanding of his rights and duties.

(iii) It develops such attitudes that makes the workers an intelligent and productive participant in economic life of the nation.

(iv) It helps the student to understand, how to purchase and use goods and services intelligently?

(v) It helps the student to understand the methods of science and scientific methods of doing business.

(vi) It makes clear to the pupil the significance of the family for the individual and the society.

(vii) It helps to develop the students capacity of appreciating the functioning of an office, business and industry.

(viii) It helps the students to develop respect for other persons.

(ix) It encourages the student to develop and maintain good health so that he can devote himself to his studies whole heartedly.

Appraisal of Curriculum of Commerce

India is a vast country and has a number of states and Union Territories. Education is in the concurrent list in Indian Constitution and so the states are free to have their independent education policies. However, following general procedure is followed for framing of curriculum in commerce by different states.

A curriculum committee is committee by the State Board or Secondary Education. The members of the committee are generally experts, who are nominated by the Board, the members meet from time to time and prescribe the courses of study and curriculum in the commerce subjects. There is also a commerce committee of university teachers which recommend the courses of study. Their recommendations are examined at various stages in the Board and then the courses of study are prescribed.

There are some defects in the system of selection of courses and curriculum in commerce stream. Experienced school tear-hers are not represented. The business circle, for which learners are prepared, are also not represented. The result is that the courses of study suffer in quality and utility.

One of the recommendation made by Kothari commission provides for the introduction of specialisation from class XI, but the boards of Secondary Education of most of the Indian states have introduced general education upto class X and specialisation from class XI. Commerce is also being incorporated as a subject of study and in several states it has already been done so in class XI and XII.

According to the growing needs of the economy and the employment opportunities available in the next decade, there is need of bringing about changes in the patterns and composition of the commerce programme. At present, of the two sequences (*i.e.* Book-keeping sequence and stenography sequence) only one sequence predominates (*i.e.* Bookkeeping sequence) and the other sequence (*i.e.* stenography sequence) remains almost neglected. Even if it has been introduced in a very few schools the programme suffers considerably on vocational grounds.

Before finalisation of any syllabus in Commerce it is desirable to have a good deal of discussion among teachers, educators, planners and administrators so that every state may adopt it, maintaining uniformity in syllabus and standard of achievement in different sequences.

Status of Commerce Education in Secondary Schools in India

In India commerce education first started at the secondary level but its real growth and development took place at the college level, upto the middle of twentieth century. In India commerce was not considered as a separate discipline and it was reduced to an insignificant item of the twin departments Economics and Commerce, in which Economics had an upper hand. It hindered any real progress in the field of commerce for a pretty long time. Only after the report of Mudaliar Commission an expansion took place in commerce education. The multipurpose Higher Secondary School were opened and practical subjects were introduced in many fields including commerce.

To start with in Commerce education were introduced such subjects as letter writing, Business Methods, Shorthand and Typewriting. Later on many more subjects such as Book-keeping Economics, Accountancy, Commercial Law, Taxation etc. were introduced. Adopting the recommendation of Dr. *V. K. R. V. Rao* Committee national Diploma in Commercial practice was started with a view to prepare qualified and skilled persons needed by the growing economy to the country.

With the rapid growth in the field of trade, commerce and industry, the need for proper education and right type of Commerce teachers was felt and to meet the needs of teachers of practical subjects a necessity was felt to have some special type of institutes. To provide for this type of institution N.C.E.R.T. and Regional Colleges of Education did a commendable job, Till about 1963 no facilities existed for providing training facilities in the field of commerce but now such training is available through regular training, in service courses, summer-cum-correspondance courses etc. but even now the practical aspect of commerce education programme is not quite satisfactory. An effort is needed to accelerate the teaching or shorthand and type-writing etc. in views of an enormously increasing demand in these fields.

There is a talk of vocationalisation and work-experience in Education. It is thus hoped that in recent future the commerce education will be much more oriented in favour of practical subjects. It would help to achieve the main objective of commerce education *i.e.* development of employable skills.

Procedure of Curriculum Construction in Commerce

All the States and Union Territories in India have their own mechanism of curriculum development. The National Council of Educational Research and Training prepares model curriculum which may be adapted/adopted by State Boards. State Boards of Education function through course committees, academic councils and the governing bodies. These committees generally comprise of principals, teachers, teacher educators and experts in the field of commerce and business.

The members of the Commerce Committee meet from time to time to lay down the course of study in different branches of Commerce. These are sent to the governing body of the State Board for approval. Thereafter these courses are circulated to the schools affiliated to the Boards.

The Central Board of Secondary Education, Delhi prescribes courses of study for schools affiliated to it. This Board is the pace setter board in the country.

CBSE Courses in Commerce

Business Studies

Overview of Commerce Courses

During the first 10 years of schooling, students are not given formal instructions in Commerce and Accountancy subjects. Hence, instructions in these two subjects should be given in such a manner that students have a good understanding of the principles and practices bearing on business, trade and industry and their relationship to society. They need to be exposed to the realities of the business world as a part of the economic, legal and social environment.

The increasing complexity of business organisation in the present day world makes it obligatory for students to be conversant with the principles and practices of management. A study of these principles will make the students aware of the functions of management in general and the purpose of management in particular activities.

The syllabus for Class XII in Business Studies comprises of two parts—Part I: "Principles and Functions of Management" is compulsory for all students while Part II is optional. The students are required to choose anyone out of the three optional parts depending on their interest and aptitude.

1. Functional Management. It specifies application of management principles in different spheres of business activities such as Personnel, Finance and Marketing. This topic is expected to be helpful to those who wish to pursue Commerce at higher level of studies.

2. Factory Organisation. It provides invaluable information and practical hints to such students who aspire to start their own small manufacturing unit in near future or they have a family business involving factory operations. A study of this topic will orient them on different aspects of setting up and organising a small scale factory unit and in handling factory routines in a small scale factory business.

3. Office Administration. It lays down specific aspects relating to an office organisation and the techniques involved in efficient handling of paper work. A study of this topic is expected to provide basic foundation knowledge to students who wish to take up a career in a business office in future.

A student offering this course is expected to be fit into routine office job with greater expertise and confidence. The topics included in the syllabus will also assist students in their higher studies.

The last two optional courses are expected to be of equal interest to girl students as women are coming in a big way for wage employment and self-employment.

Specific Objectives

Compulsory Course

1. To develop in the student an interest in the theory and practice in business, trade and industry.

2. To acquaint students with the theoretical foundations and practice of organising, managing and handling routine operations of a business firm;

3. To inculcate attitudes and values leading to the integration of business with the social system with a positive approach.

Optional Courses

1. ***Option I.*** To enable them to apply the principles and functions of management to specific aspects of business.

2. ***Option II.*** To equip them with essential fundamental knowledge for setting up, organising and handling routine operations of a small scale factory.

3. ***Option III.*** To equip them with basic information on modern methods of office operations for effectively carrying out paper work in a business office.

Accountancy

An important vehicle for communicating business information of financial nature, Accounting enables a businessman to effective measure the results of his business activities. It provides useful information to parties interested in the working of a business organisation such as management, employees, creditors, investors, Government etc. It also offers a variety of career avenues in the field of wage employment and self-employment.

Optional. Following optional areas are expected to provide knowledge and understanding in the fields of analysis of financial statements, costing and auditing. Students can choose anyone out of the three optional topics depending on their interest and aptitude.

1. *Option I.* Analysis of financial statements can be viewed as an application of the basic accounting principles for better understanding of financial statements. Its knowledge is of extreme importance to managers in arriving at important decisions relating to financial health of a business unit.

2. *Option II.* Costing as a branch of accounting provides vital information to businessmen on different aspects of cost computation.

Those who intend to run a small scale factory unit will find study of costing useful to them.

3. *Option III.* Auditing provides fundamental information on detection and correction of errors and frauds in financial accounting. Its knowledge is useful to those students who wish to engage in financial aspects of business activities.

Specific Objectives

Compulsory Course

1. To impart knowledge of methods considered useful in maintaining records of proprietary and partnership firms, companies and non-trading organisations.

2. To generate and promote awareness of students in modern techniques of maintaining accounting records with the help of computers.

Optional Courses

1. Option I. To enable students prepare financial statements and interpret results for decision making.

2. Option II. To acquaint the students with practice and procedure of determination of cost from the view point of its elements.

3. Option III. To create an awareness of the necessity of auditing for detection/rectification of errors/frauds in the process of accounting.

Commerce Course-Indian Certificate of Secondary Education Examination (ICSE)

Objectives

1. To create an awareness of the environment within which the business activity takes place.
2. To develop knowledge and understanding of the meaning and importance of Commerce.
3. To expose the students to certain technical terms in Commerce.
4. To understand the various hindrances of trade and to appreciate the aids that remove these hindrances.
5. To understand the way in which changes in the environment influence business activities.

Improvement of the Present Curriculum

Need of Diversification. It pointed out that the course content failed to keep pace with the changes in social, political, economic and industrial conditions. Theory and practice courses were theoretical and bookish and had little stuff to attract the students.

In 1934 The Sapro Committee pin-pointed introduction of diversified courses of studies to solve the problem of unemployment.

The diversified courses of study should include the following seven groups:

(i) Humanities, *(ii)* Sciences, *(iii)* Technical subjects, *(iv)* Commercial subjects, *(v)* Agricultural subjects, *(vi)* Fine arts, and *(vii)* Home Sciences.

Commerce has been introduced at high or higher secondary schools on the basic of this organisation of the syllabus.

The content courses were reorganised after the Mudaliar Commission Report. Commerce occupied an eminent, position among the vocational groups.

Imperative Needs of the Students

1. Development of Saleable Skills. The course content in the commerce programme should be arranged in such a way and so designed that it is capable of developing saleable skills among students and such attitudes that make the worker an intelligent and productive participant in economic life of the country. The student should be provided with supervised work experience and skills knowledge of their occupations.

2. Civic Development. All students must understand the rights and duties of the citizens of a democratic society, and be diligent and competent in carrying out their obligations as a member. of the community, state and the nation.

3. Business Skill. All students must know-how to purchase and use goods and service intelligently, understand both the values received by the consumer and economic consequence of their acts.

4. Family Life. All students must understand the significance of the family for the individual and the society and the conditions that are conducive for successful family life.

5. Dovelopment of Capacities. All students need opportunities to develop their capacities to appreciate the functioning of an office, business and an industry.

6. Importance of Science. All students must understand the methods of science and scientific methods of doing business transactions.

7. Training. All students should be trained in the use of their leisure time well and to budget their time wisely and balance their activities which yields satisfactions to the individual.

8. Rational Development. All students must grow their ability to think rationally and express their thoughts clearly.

9. Moral Development. All students must develop respect for other persons and grow an insight into ethical values and life co-operatively.

10. Physical Health and Fitness. All students must develop and maintain good health and physical fitness so that they can devote their attention to their studies.

Categories of Course Content

A. Vocational Commerce Education. It should consist of the following:

1. Stenographic and Secretarial Works.
2. Book-keeping and Accounting Works.
3. Clerical and general office work.
4. Office practice works—handling labour saving machines.

B. General Commerce Education. It should consist of the following concepts:

1. Consumer information—guidance.
2. Understanding of business and its management.
3. Understanding of economic systems within the country as well as outside. (Study of Economics).
4. Study of the environment, regions, nations and the world (Study of Commercial Geography).

Suggested Curriculum in Commerce

According to the growing needs of the economy and the employment opportunities available in the next decade, there is the need of bringing about great changes in the pattern and composition of the existing course contents of the commerce programme. A good deal of new thinking has been initiated on the point of the role of the commerce curriculum by the Government of India, planning commission, educationist, magnets in the field of commerce and last but not the least the Board of Secondary Examination as well as board of Secondary Education in every state in India.

At present, though there are two sequences : Book-keeping sequence and the stenographic sequence; only former sequence predominates. The stenographic sequence has been mostly ignored. Even if it has been introduced in a very few schools the programmes suffer considerably on vocational grounds.

The above four sequences may be offered at the high or higher secondary levels. They will be able to meet the future needs and demands of the youth and the society.

In order to finalise the curriculum of the commerce programme, a good deal of discussion is vitally needed among the teachers, educators, planners and administrators, so that every state may maintain uniformity in the syllabus and standards of achievement in different sequences.

Multi-Purpose School Syllabus

Even after the adoption of diversified courses in commerce it was observed that the products of commerce schools and colleges face acute problems of unemployment. After reviewing the position in India it was suggested that a student of commerce must have a general knowledge of the programmes of commerce with specialisation in one or two subjects. The students should be given a freedom to offer their subject of choice. They should be asked to take up the study of other subjects of commerce stream to acquire a general knowledge of all the subjects. Thus, improving his understanding of commerce.

Defects of Syllabus of Book-keeping

1. The syllabus of Book-keeping does not create a confidence to the business world about the ability and competency of students. It is mainly due to negligence in developing proper concepts of Book-keeping before teaching to students about : *(i)* Personal account, *(ii)* Real account, and *(iii)* Nominal account. The teacher wrong presumes that students have the knowledge of accounts.

2. In existing syllabus of book-keeping teaching starts with too many concepts by giving only a preview or general background of these concepts. It leads to utter confusion. The student fails to understand the basic concepts of book-keeping. The present syllabus is too narrow and too theoretical. So the students fail to do well in their practical life.

Improvement of Syllabus of Elements of Commerce

1. The existing syllabus is more theoretical. It fails to develop the skills of handling business activities. It should pin point various equipments that a school must have for proper teaching of the subject. The possession of these teaching aids should be mandatory for the schools.

2. The existing text-books should be modified so as to include the important areas of business. They should also include the up-to-date procedure of export, import licensing and Banking etc.

3. The practical training in commercial office, business office, bank etc. be made compulsory. The syllabus must have certain basic concepts *e.g.* mock trails, group discussions, projects etc.

Improvement of Syllabus of Economics

1. The existing syllabus fails to train the students in applied economics. The main objective of teaching economics is to develop economic understanding of the functions of production, consumption, exchange and distribution for making the individual and society 'better' and 'among other things' promote the general welfare and preserve democratic ideals. The knowledge of applied branch of economics is a must to achieve such an objective. A paper in economics must cover the following:

(i) Various objectives of five year plans of India.

(ii) The Industrial policy of Government of India and its impact on Indian Economy.

(iii) Agricultural contribution to the Indian Economy.

(iv) Export-import trade in India.

(v) Foreign trade policy of Indian Government.

2. The syllabus needs a thorough screening and framed in such a way as to develop business economics understanding in the student. It should also aim to develop students' understanding and appreciation of role, the business plays in our daily life.

5

Teaching Methods of Commerce

There are two view points about teaching methods. According to one every teacher should have knowledge of various teaching methods. The second view point is that if the teacher has full knowledge of the subject-matter, then he need not know or use any method. Here, the first view point gives a great importance to teaching methods. Really speaking both the view points are defective. For successful teaching the teacher should have adequate knowledge of both *i.e.,* the subject-matter and teaching methods. With the reconciliation of the two only; success of teaching will be possible.

Binning & Binning, "If teaching is to reach its highest degree of efficiency, it is evident that teachers must be thoroughly trained in material instruction in their fields and must also possess a broad understanding of all phases of method—including psychology—as a part of that philosophy of education which is essential to good teaching."

The term, 'Method' in education is used to refer to those processes of the teacher, through which the pupil learns the knowledge of the subject-matter. The importance of the teaching method in respect of a subject is similar to the right path leading to the set destination.

According to *John Dewey,* "Method is a way of managing to develop conclusion."

According to *E.B. Wesley*, "Method of teaching in education refers to the series of activities for guidance adopted by the teacher, which transform into learning on the part of the pupils."

So, the method is not an activity, but is a process which does not confine to anyone step, but is created by linking many steps and their balanced form gives rise to a method.

Importance of Teaching Method

It is necessary for the teacher to have knowledge of right methods.

The Secondary Education Commission 1952, writes in the report, "Even the best curriculum and the most perfect syllabus remains dead unless quickened into life by the right methods of teaching and the right kind of teachers."

Mrs. S.K. Kochhar, in her book, *'Method and Technique of Teaching'* has beautifully interpreted the importance of teaching methods. She writes, "A teacher must be fully conversant with the different methods of teaching in the same way as a soldier is to be conversant with the various weapons of fighting. Which methods he should use at a particular time depends upon his judgement."

Thus the teaching methods are very important in the teaching-learning process. Teaching methods make teaching systematic and simple. It is necessary for all teachers to have the knowledge of teaching methods. Teaching methods are closely related with the aims and values of education and help in achieving them. Teaching methods are very important in teaching work, but the teacher should use them very carefully. To drag all, with the same staff is improper. In the same way it is equally unsuitable to teach all subjects or to teach all pupils with one and the same method. The teacher should alter methods in accordance with subject-matter, the needs and aptitudes of pupils. In education, the teaching method should not be confined to a certain stable aspect.

According to *Binning & Binning*, "Methodology should be conceived as a dynamic function of education and not as a static aspect of the process of teaching."

At the same time while using teaching methods, the teacher should keep in mind his own aptitudes and abilities. He should see that he possesses such aptitudes and abilities which enable him to use a rnodem method. The teacher should make the method his servant. If a method does not work successfully owing to particular reasons, then the teacher should abandon that method and should adopt any other method. For this the teacher should know all teaching methods. In the words of *Binning & Binning*, "The successful teacher is he who them is familiar with all the methods and who them, with his aims clearly in view selects the method that will best aid him in attaining them."

The above account makes it clear that to teach a subject-matter successfully, teaching methods are very important and these methods are closely related to aims and values of education.

Characteristics of Good Method

Good methods used in teaching, have the following characteristics:

1. These are helpful in achieving pre-determined aims and objectives.
2. A method should be such as to inspire pupils for activity and self study.
3. The method should be defmite and suitable for that particular topic and class.
4. A method should be such as to make pupils active participants in the teaching learning process.

5. A good method is dynamic.

   The method should include adequate activities so as to enable pupils for self expression.

6. A good method is practical. It enables the teacher to know what is desirable and what is not.

7. A good method develops in pupils, reasoning, decision making, analytical faculty and fully takes cognisance of individual differences.

On the basis of above stated features, the teacher plays the role of a guide. The subject-matter and teaching method should be determined from the point of view of the pupil.

Methods of Teaching Commerce

After selecting the subject-matter, it becomes the duty of the teacher to see how it may be taught and learnt. This can be possible only by using effective methods. Following are the main types of methods.

Question-Answer Method. In Question-Answer method of teaching commerce the teacher puts the questions to the pupils while the answers given by the pupils are supplemented and elaborated by him. In asking questions, the relevant experiences in the memory of the students come to the surface and the familiar and known association help in learning and granting the unfamiliar and the unknown. The pupils readjust the old for acquiring new knowledge. As the old and the new get integrated the process of learning commerce becomes simpler and easier.

In this method the teacher puts questions to the pupils to motivate them and create a felt need for learning something new or solve some new problems. In the beginning questions are asked directly about such past experiences of the pupils which are relevant to the present lesson. They are put in a manner that the present topic appears to the pupils as a problem in whose solution they may be naturally interested. These are generally developmental questions both the narrative and developmental questions are used in the presentation stage. It seeks the solution to the problem developed during the preparation or introduction stage. In the recapitulation or application stage, questions are asked to find out the grasp of the subject-matter or to help the pupils apply the knowledge granted to new situations. Thus, learning is consolidated and insight deepened.

Advantages. The question-answer procedure develops the pupil's insight into the lesson. It leads to the understanding and comprehension of the subject-matter presented.

The question-answer method ensures active participation of the pupils.

Supported by different visual aids like pictures, charts, films, filmstrips, etc., and devices like dramatisation in different forms this method can go a long way in sustaining the interest of the pupils.

Conversational Method. This method follows the question-answer technique. While the teacher puts the questions to the pupils, the answers given by the latter lead to the development of the lesson. The teacher supplements and elaborates the answers of the pupils from time to time. By asking questions, the relevant past experiences come to the fore. The familiar and known association help in learning and grasping the unfamiliar and unknown. The pupils readjust the old and the new to integrate it and to simply the process of learning commerce.

Procedure

1. Preparation Stage. During the preparation stage, questions are asked directly on past experiences of the pupils relevant to the present lesson in a way that the present lesson appears as a problem in whose solution pupils are naturally interested. These questions are generally developmental.

2. Application Stage. In this stage questions are asked to help pupils apply the knowledge gained to new situations to consolidate and deepen insight.

3. Presentation Stage. In the presentation stage, both the narrative and developmental questions are used to solve the problem developed during the preparation stage. This procedure develops pupils insight into the lesson. It leads to the learning of the subject-matter presented.

Advantages. The conversational method or Question-Answer method is a good method of teaching commerce. It should be supported by visual aids like pictures, charts, models, films, filmstrips and devices like dramatisation in different forms. Thus, this ensures interest of the pupils and learning becomes an interesting experience.

Reasons for Use

1. Unsuitable Text-books. One of the reasons for the use of this method by most of our commerce teachers is the absence of suitable text-books. In text-books, while some topics are magnified beyond proportion as they have some individual appeal for the author, other topics receive only scanty treatment. The language of most of the text-books is tough. As the text-books meant for school children are written by university and college professors neither having experience of teaching youngsters nor being conversant with their psychological needs, the reading material is tough and beyond the comprehension of average students. These teachers start dictating notes to get speedy results.

2. Shortage of Time. As the curriculum in commerce is overcrowded the commerce teacher looks for a short-cut-dictation of notes to finish the course in time.

3. Fatigue. In our schools a commerce teacher is generally overburdened with work. As he is expected to take more than thirty periods in a week he does not get enough time for preparation. If he is allotted some period towards the fag-end of the day most of the pupils are already tired due to strenuous work put in the preceding periods, in such exacting subjects as Mathematics, English etc.

5. Teachers Lacking Power of Expression. Commerce teachers which lack the power of expression can neither narrate nor lecture well. Therefore, they resort to note-dictation saving the trouble of making preparation for narration or lecture.

Style of Notes Dictation

1. Notes on Important Topic Only. Some teachers give detailed notes on important topics only such as cold war, technological development, international peace, and cooperation, new economic order, Fascism and Nazism etc. As a normal practice, these notes are given, when the teacher has already discussed the topics in the class.

2. Substance on Blackboard. After explaining the topic in detail some teachers give notes in the form of substance on the black-board.

They also require the pupils to prepare the lesson at home in advance. They are asked only to copy the substance from the black-board.

3. Question-Answer. Teachers who give notes in the question-answer from select important and expected questions and dictate answers.

Disadvantages of Dictating Notes

1. No Use of Critical Power. Note dictated obstruct the use of critical powers, which is one of the important aims of teaching commerce. Taking the matter dictated by the teacher as gospel truth a pupil crams it without testing the relevance of the material.

2. No Insight in the Subject. Pupils fail to develop the habit of consulting reference books; Disregarding the text-books they fail to develop proper insight into the subject.

3. Based on the False Principle. It is based on the false principle that instruction is a process of memorisation. This commerce teaching is made synonymous with the memorisation of facts communicated by the teacher.

Thus, the pupils should think and express, consult all possible good works on the subject and prepare their own notes in commerce.

Observation Method. Importance. Immediate surroundings and community afford many opportunities for observation. Concrete tangible, visible and describable data on cultural, industrial, political and geographic facts and relationships prove invaluable for the teaching of commerce. Observation lends vitality to the subject-matter of commerce. Direct experiences are more effective in the process of learning they are also retained for a longer period of time. As rich, full-bodied purposeful experiences seen, handled, tasted, touched, felt and smelled. They are the unabridged version of life itself. A trip to a monument, a fort, a temple, an institution, provides its first-hand experiences which are real. The children can see them, ask questions about them and examine them. Such experiences are highly conducive to learning.

Advantages. Under the careful guidance of commerce teacher's observation provides the pupils ample opportunities for asking questions, gathering data and .pooling information. Visit to telephone exchanges, newspaper and telegraph offices clarify ideas about communication. Study trips to airports and other transportation centres show how people and goods are moved about. Production and consumption can be understood better when pupils see the stores, the markets and factories of the community.

Techniques of Observation

1. Field Trips. Field trips are undertaken for securing information, changing attitudes, awakening interests, developing appreciation, promoting ideas and enjoying new experiences. Used to initiate a unit of study; they may be a part of its core and they can give it the final touch.

2. Community Service Projects. Community service projects involve individual activity of an integrated, mental, physical, emotional and spiritual nature. They are of genuine educational value to the pupil as well as to the society.

3. Community Surveys. Community surveys foster comprehensive understanding of community structure and processes in their everyday operation, interaction and complexity. In stimulating depth of insight into vital community problems and trends which have been influenced by past conditions, present developments and future prospects community surveys are very useful.

There can be no difficulty in preparing a catalogue of the available resources for proper and detailed study if the teacher is resourceful and the class is enthusiastic and clever. The resources which need to be observed by the pupils vary from community to community. There may be classified under various heads such as resources of geographical, historical, cultural, economic and scientific interests. For the observation of the resources leading maximum benefit to the pupils proper procedure should be followed.

Discussion Method

One of the most valuable methods of teaching commerce is discussion. It is said, "two heads are better than one".

Wonderful results are achieved when a number of heads combine to solve a problem.

Advantages

1. This method is best for a problem, an issue or a situation in which there a difference of opinion. In the discussion method of teaching commerce there is exchange of opinion accompanied by a search for its factual basis.
2. If agreement is not reached, discussion has the value of clarifying and sharpening the nature of agreement.
3. Speech is free and responsible. Values are created not quarrelled about. The participants are engaged in a process of competitive cooperation. Agreement is the declared purpose of discussion which is an ordered process of collective decision-making.

Objectives of Discussion

As a method of teaching commerce discussion may be used for the following objectives:

(i) To lay plans for new work;

(ii) To make decisions concerning future action;

(iii) To obtain and gaining respect for various points of view;

(iv) To clarify ideas;

(v) To share information;

(vi) To inspire interest; and

(vii) To evaluate progress.

Steps in Discussion

1. In the case of problems:

(i) Locating and defining problems of common interest and significance;

(ii) Working together to find ways of solving the problems;

(iii) Evaluating the effectiveness of the suggested solutions and their implementations;

(iv) Allocating responsibilities for the solutions suggested.

2. In case of plans for projects and programmes:

(i) Deciding on the programme and the particulars such as date time and place;

(ii) Enumerating the jobs to be done in organising the programme;

(iii) Allocating duties to the members of the group; and

(iv) Evaluating the results.

Forms of Discussion

1. Debate. In the programme of debate two or more students holding contradictory opinions present arguments on a particular problem. They also rebut the opposite side. Finally the rest of the class is encouraged to ask questions from the debaters or engage in a brief discussion with them. A debate requires a moderator. The teacher should work both with the debaters and the class in order to get significant results.

2. Symposium. In a symposium the participants present to the audience through speeches or proper reading their views about various aspects of a selected problem or topic. To quote Struck, "We think of a symposium as a group of comments, either spoken or written, which portrays contrasting or at least different points of view". The objective of the symposium is to clarify thoughts upon controversial questions. The audience listens to the discussion. Each person forms his own conclusions concerning the validity of the points of view presented. The ideal number of pupil participants in a symposium is four or five.

3. Panel Discussions. It is a discussion among a selected group persons, large enough for variety and small enough for purposeful deliberations. The ideal number may be four to six persons. The participants in a panel discussion are usually eminent persons in their fields. They present various points of view before an audience which subsequently joins in the discussion. The purpose of panel discussion is to get important facts from different angles, to stimulate thinking and lay a basis for wide participation. No speeches are made by the members among them only informal conversations take place.

Advantages

Panel discussion method provides a natural setting in which people get the opportunity to ask questions, to evaluate replies and to contribute constructively.

4. Brain Storming. In this form of discussion the brains of the participants are stimulated to create a storm of ideas and give suggestions regarding the topic without any deliberation to find whether or not they are meaningful and purposeful. When the brain is let go thus without social institutions, it would be able to give expressions to some of the most useful and practical suggestions. For example, "Small saving could do a lot to strengthen the savings movement" is a good subject for brain storming.

Procedure of Discussion

1. Planning. To make proper use of the discussion method the teacher and student representatives should do considerable planning. In planned and well-directed procedure discussion the whole process may be divided into three stages—preparation, discussion and evaluation.

2. Conducting. The conducting the discussion should be disciplined. The arrangement of seats should ensure face-to-face talk. The strength of the discussion is obtained from the information and viewpoint of all members of the group. All should contribute to its progress as it is a thinking-together process which breaks-down if one member of the group dominates it. Ensuring that every member to the group participates the teacher should encourage sincere questions and comments. He must gear the discussion to the realisation of specific objectives and development of proper skills and methods.

3. Preparation. For through preparation for the discussion the teacher should read wide and deep purposefully and critically and prepare the material conscientiously. Arranged logically points to be discussed should be written on the chalk board for guidance. If the students do not initially feel the need of the problem to be discussed they should be made to do so.

4. Evaluation. Discussion results in expanding information or lessening or removing prejudices, changing attitudes or ideals, increasing the range of interest, altering ideas concerning national and international policies, or causing a member to become a more active citisen. One must evaluate the discussion with these motives in mind.

Advantages of Discussion

***(i)* Useful Both for the Juniors and Seniors.** Junior children learn through conversation and discussion, to take turns, listen attentively, act cooperatively, speak distinctly, stand and sit correctly, respect the ideas of others, share interests, ask pertinent questions, utilise simple information and comprehend the problem before the group. Senior children plan and discuss problems with the entire group and in smaller units. The group learns together and presents important information, makes suggestions, shares responsibility, comprehends the topic, evaluates the findings and summarises results.

***(ii)* Increase in Knowledge.** Through discussion children crystallise their thinking and identify concepts needing further study. Therefore, their knowledge of commerce becomes clear.

***(iii)* Moderation.** Through discussion students know and understand that difference in perspective need not result in disaster and that people may believe in the same thing for different reasons.

***(iv)* Clarification and Sharpening of the Issues.** In discussion new ground is discovered both for agreement and disagreement. Old ideas and values may be replaced by new ones.

***(v)* Knowledge of Limitations.** The student discovers what he did not know, what he has overlooked and wherein he was mistaken both as to facts and the method of interpreting them. He may find out what he knows and the surety with which he knows it.

***(vi)* Helpful in Establishing an Attitude of Looking Forward to Progress and Growth.** Self-evaluation discussion activates thinking along the lines of self-evaluation.

***(vii)* Discovering Leaders.** Discussion helps the teacher in discovering students with a potential for becoming genuine leaders.

***(viii)* Intellectual Team Work.** Discussion represents a type of intellectual team-work resting on the principle that the pooled knowledge, ideas and feelings of several persons have greater merit than those of a single individual.

***(ix)*Tolerance.** Discussion engenders toleration for views which are at variance, from those one holds.

Unit Method. It is a new experiment in education, to teach subject-matter methodically in the form of units.

It is based upon *Gestalt* psychology. According to it our attention is drawn *(i)* to the object in its whole form, and *(ii)* we accept one object in place of another. So, the second object becomes the basis for the first one. So after full attention is focussed on the whole object, attention is then given, to its parts. Just as, when a person comes to us, his entire picture is drawn upon and later on attention goes to the different parts of his body.

Thus, with reference to education the pupils attention is readily engaged by the whole form of the subject matter and subsequently to other elements. Hence, the teacher should, in the process of teaching while presenting every topic in a serial order use Unit Method in lesson platting and thereby should make teaching natural and effective.

Different educators have accepted 'Unit Method' as a purposeful organisation of activities which is related to some or another in the first instance the object is presented in the whole form and subsequently relation is established with experiences, activities and conduct. Thus, the Unit Method helps in making teaching process clear, effective and useful.

H.C. Mormon, "Unit is a comprehensive and significant aspect of the environment, of an organised science, of an art, or of conduct which on being learnt results in an adaptation of personality.

According to *Thomas M. Risk,* "The term 'Unit' signifies the unity or wholeness of learning activities relating to some problems or project."

N.C.E.R.T. "A unit is an instructional device which gives knowledge to students in a composite manner."

G.V. Good. "Unit is a major sub-division of course of study, a text-book or a subject field, particularly a sub-division of Commerce, practical arts or science also. It is an organisation of various activities, experiences and types of learning around a central theme, problem or purpose, developed cooperatively by a group of pupils-teacher leadership. It involves planning, execution of plan and evaluation of results."

James M. Lee, "A unit is the general content process frame-work for the learning of the various inter-related facts of the topic or problem. Hence a unit is a pattern of organisation, not a method of teaching.

Above definitions are not entirely accepted because no one definition has been evolved so far as may be acceptable to all educators.

Steps of Unit Method

Some scholars have made efforts to present unit technique in the form of a teaching method. To make it useful for class teaching. Morrison advocates five steps. Risk advocates three steps in this method. The separate analysis of teaching steps as given by the two scholars is given as under. Risk writes, "The unit plan teaching technique consists simply the following of the major psychological steps in developing a unit. "He gave the following three steps of Unit teaching:

(a) Introducing the units and devices

(b) Developing the unit

(c) Culminating the unit

Morrison advocate the following five steps in unit teaching:

1. ***Exploration.*** In this stage, the teacher ascertains how much previous knowledge the pupils have, relating to the new unit. The teacher can ascertain the previous knowledge of pupils using the following devices and ways:

   (a) Written test,

   (b) Through oral questions, and

   (c) By exchange of views.

2. ***Presentation.*** At this stage the teacher presents the subject-matter through conversation or narration. Subsequently; with the help of questioning he ascertains if the pupils have grasped the subject-matter of the unit. If they have not understood it the teacher will again present the same. He will move to the next step after the pupils have demonstrated that they have understood the unit.

3. ***Organisation.*** In this stage pupils organise knowledge, by systematically writing the subject-matter of the unit. If they succeed in doing so, the teacher takes for granted, that the pupils have thoroughly understood the subject-matter of the unit.

4. ***Assimilation.*** Pupils are give opportunity to digest the subject-matter of the unit. At this stage, the pupils, can assimilate the subject-matter through the following medium:

   (i) By studying

   (ii) By writing

   (iii) By talking to each other, and

   (iv) Consultation with the teacher.

Thus, this method takes the mixed form of 'supervised study' and "laboratory method'.

5. ***Recitation.*** Now the pupils are in a position to recite all or important portions. This step is important for giving training to speak.

Binning and Binning are of the view that the steps of Morrison plan were made for units in science. But with some improvement or modification these can be used in teaching at Commerce. They wrote, while appreciating Morrison plan, "On evaluation of the process of Meristem, it comes to the knowledge easily that he made use of modern principles of education and the elements of teaching."

Discussion Unit Method. Discussion unit method is one of the various teaching methods of Commerce. It is such a method which engages pupils mentally and physically in activities relating to education and enables them to adjust with new situations.

It is a system which makes teaching and learning effective. It is a means of instruction which brings about important modifications in pupils, by offering knowledge and experience. The extensive material of Commerce is divided into main divisions and each such division is called a unit. Each related until should be so small as to enable pupils to easily understand it. A Unit can bring important modifications in pupils, in the form of knowledge and experiences which are integrated.

Characteristics of Discussion Unit Method

The following are the features of the discussion unit method:

1. The unit should be experimental.
2. The unit should be related with the entire syllabus.

3. Unit should be coordinated with social emotional and educational activities.

4. Unit must be divided into smaller units so that the lesson becomes easier and clear.

5. While framing the unit, attention should be paid to the level, class and time, at our disposal.

6. Unit should neither be too small nor should it be too big.

7. Unit must be based on pupil's previous knowledge.

8. Unit should be in the nature of guidance to the pupils.

9. Unit must be in accordance with the interest, needs and mental level of pupils.

Merits of Discussion Unit Method

1. It pays attention to the individual interest and problems of the child. Hence it does not insist on similar progress of success of all pupils. In it pupils get education in accordance with their individual differences.

2. In this method there is no specialisation of knowledge attempted, but the syllabus is fully generalised and presented before the pupils.

3. This method has, not only the teachers' lecture and the text-book, but other supplementary material is also appropriately used.

4. It trains in systematised deliberation and establishes relationships.

5. There is flexibility in it and as such full attention can be given to individual differences. The unit imparts knowledge of the entire lesson.

6. It develops logical thinking.
7. It develops in pupils proper aptitudes and interests and it develops social relationship amongst pupils.

Demerits of Discussion Unit Method

1. It intraps pupils 'in futile discussion, owing to which time and efforts become wasteful'. Noise and disorder continues to prevail in the class.
2. It is difficult to finish the entire syllabus in time, due to which often knowledge remains unclear and incomplete.
3. Shy pupils, hesitate taking part in the discussion and owing to which talkative pupils overshadow the discussion.
4. The success of this method depends upon efficient and trained teachers of which, unfortunately there is a great dearth.

Assignment Method. Assignment method is advocated for the teaching of commerce in higher classes. Where the whole of the syllabus is split into significant topics or units and each topic or unit is sub-divided into assignments. The pupils prepare the assignments in writing. This helps in organisation of knowledge, assimilation of facts and better preparation for examinations.

Types of Assignments

1. Preparatory Assignments. Through these assignments meant for circulation the pupils can be prepared for the work which is to follow on the next day. This preliminary pilot work enables the teacher to lead the class with ease and understanding.

2. Study Assignments. These include problem-solving assignments, assignments on making and handling tools, assignments on picture reading, assignments for the preparation of a topic in the light of references provided.

Following are some problem-solving assignments:

(i) ***Solving Problems of a Mathematical Nature.*** With an average speed of 500 miles per hour a jet air-liner is going round the world on a non-stop flight. How many hours will take to complete a flight *(i)* along the tropic of cancer and *(ii)* along the 30 N latitude.

(ii) ***Searching for Causes.*** A traveller resolved to go round the world in 80 days. He reached 5 minutes late and was sorry about it. However, his friends told him that they were surprised to see him reach there a day in advance.

(iii) ***Assignments on Making and Handling Tools.*** These include assignments of taking readings, and maintaining records. Converting recorded data into geographical tools for better and clearer understanding, preparing simple and interesting geographical tools, preparing models and charts, interpreting graphs, charts and cartograms.

(iv) ***Assignments on Picture.*** These include assignments on picture-reading as review revision through pictures, correlating a picture with a plan, an air view, or a map, matching pictures and places, clarifying concepts through pictures, selecting and appreciating the best pictures, etc.

(v) ***Remedial Assignments.*** Revised in the light of pupil's reactions to the three types of assignments mentioned above, the purpose of these assignments is to remove weak points and clear misunderstandings.

(vi) ***Creative Assignment.*** These include assignments for listing points in favour of, or against a given

argument, reaching valid conclusions from statistical or visual data, writing letters, dialogues imaginary travelogues and autobiographical accounts of imaginary situations, etc.

(vii) Revisional Assignments. Keeping in view the specific objectives of the subject-matter being tested these assignments are worked out in advance. These include assignments for *(a)* providing drill to the work done by the students, and *(b)* for checking their retention and reproduction of facts, incidents, etc., of the topic and *(c)* for checking the understanding of the topic.

Parts of Assignment Lesson

1. Preparation. In preparation efforts are made for developing the pupils interest in writing the assignment. This work can be completed in one period. Broadheads should be outlined under which the assignment is to be written. The necessary information, including the references, etc. be given which would help the pupils in working out the assignment.

2. Writing. This work may take more than one class period. The pupils may write the assignment at home or in the class. If they write in assignment in the class under the supervision of the teacher, they should be allowed the facilities to consult books and ask questions whenever necessary.

3. Teachers Work. This includes correction of sample assignment scripts by the teacher and preparation of common list of errors.

4. Selection of Pairs for Mutual Corrections. To help them in correction work the pupils may be given a list of the types of probable errors occurring in writing commerce assignments such as omission of vital facts, wrong statement of facts, statement of irrelevant facts, failure to bring out causal relationships, etc.

5. Correction by Pupils. Now the pupils may be asked to correct their assignments at home.

6. Discussion of the List in a Correction Class. Finally the common errors committed by the pupils should be discussed in a correction class to check their recurrence.

Advantages of Assignment

1. Teachers Knowing the Interests of his Pupils in a Particular Subject-area. He is also able to discover the specific abilities of the individual pupil which may be developed and used for their own good.

2. Suitability. The method is quite suitable for pupils of different ability levels such as gifted, average and slow learners.

3. Teachers Foreseeing of the Difficulties which the Students may have to Face in the Learning of the Topic. The teacher can guide the pupils by intelligently putting thought-provoking questions in his assignments. The question and guidance to read or to study a topic will prepare the pupils to face the difficulties boldly.

Problem Solving Method. It is not entirely a new method. Its use was made by ancient thinkers—like Socrates. But modem times, teachers and thinkers have accepted it as educational means. In it, mental conclusions are given more importance and there is deliberation and criticism. So, *George Johnson* writes, "The best course to train the mind is to present before the students real problems and for the solution of which opportunities and freedom are to be made available."

In modern times, some people accept the Problem solving method as a technique and others as a teaching method. *Clark* and *Stone* write, "None of us should call Problem Solving as a technique." This method tries to frode out solution scientifically of specific problem or difficulty. To explain its meaning, some definitions are given below.

Carter V. Good, "Problem method is a method of instruction by which learning is stimulated by the creation of challenging situations that demand solution."

John Dewey, "The real problem is contained in the fact which, though seemingly appear trifle and ordinary, yet makes the mind restless and challenging, rendering belief uncertain."

James M. Lee, "Problem solving is an educational device whereby the teacher-pupils attempt at a conscious, planned, purposeful efforts to arrive at an explanation or solution to some educationally significant difficulty. Problem-solving is general educational method rather than a specific pedagogical technique."

Elements of Problem Method

1. Problems should be practical and useful.
2. It should have educational utility.
3. It should be in accordance with the needs and (physical and mental) aptitudes of the pupils.
4. Its nature should be clear and definite.
5. It should be related to social and physical environment.

Steps in Problem Method

1. Selection of the Problem. The teacher and the pupils should together select the problem to be studied. It is necessary to get pupils' cooperation, all the more, because good results will not be achieved, unless they own up the problem. While selecting the problem, the teacher and the pupils should keep the following points in mind:

- The problem should be real.
- The problem should be important from the educational point of view.
- The problem should be suitable for situation. Necessary instructions must be available therein.
- In other words let the problem offer to pupils opportunities to learn.
- The problem should be related to the unit of the syllabus.

2. Why is it a Problem? After the selection of the problem, let the teacher induce the pupils to know why at all it is a problem? If there is only one answer to a question, then it cannot be a problem. For a problem, alternatives are a must. So, let the pupils see what different alternatives are present in the problem.

3. Finding out the Solution of the Problem. Pupils after collecting the required material, will find out some solution of the problem. This will be based upon established tested facts and principles. At the same time it will be clear and certain.

4. Carrying out the Problem. The entire class will work for the solution of the problem under the direction of the teacher. How to solve the problem? The decision will depend upon the nature of the problem *e.g.* if the nature of the problem is inductive, then inductive steps will be followed. If its nature is deductive, the steps concerning the same will be followed. So, according to the nature of the problem, pupils will collect relevant information. Subsequently, they will organise and analyse the same. The teachers' guidance will not be there to tell the solution, but will be related to its search and study needs besides difficulties to be tackled individually and collectively by the pupils.

5. Application of the Solution. The pupils should apply this solution in life, in the form of the class and individually. If they do not do so, they will be unable to adopt it in their own life and the work done by them in the school will be futile.

Merits of Problem Method

1. Pupils learn to tackle social problems of their future life.
2. They learn to collect facts and organise them properly.
3. It helps in awakening respect for mutual views and the feeling of toleration.
4. Scientific outlook develops in pupils.
5. It encourages them for self study and develops interest for extra and complementary study.
6. They do not depend on blind imitation and on the habit of rote memory.
7. It develops self-reliance, confidence, self-study habits in pupils.
8. Pupils receive proper training for using the material in books and periodicals and find out truth and falsehood.
9. The pupils always remain active.
10. It develops pupils' mental faculty-reason, concept and contemplation and imagination.
11. It saves pupils from becoming prey to prejudices/ bias.

Demerits of Problem Method

1. It is not useful for pupils at primary level, and can only be used in high classes.
2. It takes too much time. As a result, the syllabus cannot be finished in time.
3. It involves much expenditure.
4. It is not necessary that this method will yield satisfactory results.
5. It cannot be used for every topic.
6. Difficult problem creates disappointment in pupils.
7. It needs experienced and capable teachers, since average teacher cannot use it.
8. It is not possible to study the subject continuously and in a serial order.

Modern Methods. Educators have fixed the development of all the facilities of students as their main aim. To achieve this aim, the educationists have developed various methods of teaching. The bases of these methods is to put on pupils the responsibility of self-learning. Every pupil has some or other aptitudes. The chief aim of modern education is to explore such aptitudes for, development. To receive instruction, pupils should have interest in it. They will acquire the knowledge of subject-matter if they have interest. Modern psychologists have pointed out that pupils receive best education:

1. Through observation and inspection.
2. By establishing relationship.
3. Through problem-solving.
4. By experimenting.

5. Through creative activity.

6. By exchange of views.

All these are useful in receiving instruction in Commerce. These methods are known as Activity Methods or Modern Methods.

Lecture Method. This method has been used in education from ancient days. At pressant also this method has occupied an important place in Indian schools. The teacher, in it, teaches through telling. It is called Telling Method. For success, the lecture method depends upon two factors:

(a) The selection of the subject-matter, and

(b) The manner of presenting the subject-matter. The mode of presentation depends upon the personality of the teacher. For this, it is necessary for him to have proper preparation and suitable voice. Some progressive thinkers in education, are of the opinion that this method of teaching is unsuitable. But this argument does not appear to be correct, since this method is not opposed to the principles of psychology. There takes place some mental activity in the pupils. With full preparation the teacher can present the subject-matter in an interesting way and can ask question to keep them active. It all depends upon the teacher how he makes use of the method. Lecture accounts for alertness of auditory faculty. The lecture, along with personality of the speaker, finds place in the minds' of the pupils.

When to use Lecture Method

The teacher can use lecture/narration method, telling method for the following purposes:

1. **To Motivate.** Before presenting a lesson or a unit of the subject, the pupils can be encouraged to study

the same, by explaining first, the important points through lecture method. With this, their learning will be facilitated when the subject-matter will be presented.

2. **To Summarise.** Some pupils are up-set on seeing the extensiveness of the subject-matter. They find themselves unsuccessful to come out of the cobweb of the subject-matter. In such a case, they do not agree to study the extensive subject-matter. Hence it is necessary that this extensive subject-matter be presented in such a way so that the whole subject-matter be presented in a small form. This task can easily be done by lecture method. In addition, by presenting the subject matter in a brief form, the pupils can be given a broad knowledge of the subject-matter. Owing to this its study becomes meaningful when they read books. So, the use of the lecture method should be made to summarise the subject-matter.

3. **To Clarify.** Lecture method can be used to explain the events, terms concepts and principles involved in the subject. It is only possible by lecture method to interpret. It is necessary to clarify them in simple words. So, lecture method can be adopted affectively.

4. **To Save Time.** It takes time to read and understand the text-book. In the same way modern methods of teaching also require time. With lecture method pupils' time can be saved. Through lecture, adequate subject-matter can be presented in short time. Hence, lecture method can be used also for saving the time of the pupils.

5. **To Present Additional Material.** At times, the subject matter may be too briefing the books and may be insufficient. Looking at the level of the pupils, the

teacher can give additional matter. So with the help of lecture method, the teacher can present additional material to pupils to add to their knowledge.

6. **To Give Assignment.** It is highly unpsychological to give home-work saying, "Write an essay on whatever you have learnt in the class. " In fact, for the usefulness of homework, a brief lecture may be delivered on it relation to present subject-matter and how it may be done etc. While giving home-work, the teacher should make use of a lecture.

Advantages of Lecture Method

1. Individualised Instruction. It is based on lecture/ narration method. The printed words in the book cannot tell much to the students. Books cannot pay attention to individual differences. But in lecture method, the teacher and the pupils sit face to face and carry out exchange of knowledge ideas. The subject-matter can adequately be made clear, as best as possible, through discussion; conversation, criticism in the course of give and take. The teacher can remove individual difficulties.

2. Development of Logical Reasoning. This method develops reasoning and expression of students. Pupils reason with the speaker and analyse and comment on the principles theories presented by him and through discussion, resolve their doubts. Thus their reasoning power develops and they learn to express their ideas.

3. Classification of Subject-Matter. In this method, the subject-matter is made clear to the maximum. Many points come up in the subject-matter which are tough and complicated. The subject remains unqualified, on one reading. Through lecture method, the unqualified points can be reapeated again and again and can be expressed in other words, till it becomes clear to pupils.

4. It Saves Time. If teaching is done by this method, it will save a lot of time and labour. Through lecturing, extensive subject-matter can be presented briefly in a short time. In the text-book method the pupils have to spend time and labour in reading the important and unimportant parts of the subject-matter. Through the lecture only the relevant subject-matter is presented in easy language, and their time and labour is saved.

5. Unit Method in Teaching of Commerce/Science. To prepare introduction of a new topic, subject or unit this method is the best. With this method, topics like nationalisation of banks, inflation, satyagrah can be explained in a short time. The points/issues become clearer through lecture method. In addition, pupils' time can also be saved.

6. Improvement in Pronunciation. It improves the pronunciation of the pupils. The pupils imitate the pronunciation of the teacher and improve their own expression.

7. To Make Subject-Matter Interesting and Effective. By this method, the teacher can make the subject interesting. In it the teacher can clarify the matter through interpretation and gestures. As compare with printed words, spoken words are more effective. At times the teacher can more effectively tell what he wants to tell to the class by his tone, gestures and facial expression.

8. Pupils and Teacher Remain Active. To some extent, both remain active. The teacher narrates and puts questions to pupils on the present problems.

9. Psychological in Nature. The teacher plans his lecture on psychological basis whereas the text-books are written on logical basis. Thus, the lectures are superior to text-books and according to child psychology.

10. Clarification of Home-work. At the end of the lesson, pupils are given home-work. Mostly pupils do not attempt it. The main reason is that they do not understand what is to be done in respect of the home-work. The teacher briefly explains the home to through lecture.

Disadvantages of Lecture Method

1. Pupils are Passive Listeners. It is not a natural method. Often the immature teacher, while lecturing, makes the pupils passive in the class. Such a teacher goes on lecturing and the pupils listen to him like statues. They do not take any interest in class teaching.

2. One Sided. From educational point of view this method is one sided. The pupil is not required to work as much as the teacher has to. In India the teacher has to deliver nearly six lectures per day. It is difficult for the teacher to prepare six lectures per day.

3. Stress on Theoretical Knowledge. It puts more emphasis on the theoretical knowledge of the subject. No importance is given to the practical part of knowledge. It does not assign any place to activity. It fully disregards, 'learning by doing' .

4. Lack of Real Knowledge. It is one thing to conduct real study and quite another to finish the syllabus. The lecture method can finish the syllabus quickly, but does not generate real learning.

5. Unstable Knowledge. Knowledge gained by this method, does not become permanent since knowledge of this type has no relation with activity and is not related to practical work.

6. Lack of Deep Study. Pupils do not get opportunity to carry out original study. They begin feeling contented with whatever subject-matter the teacher presents. Pupils do not learn to develop habits of self-study.

7. Limited Time. The attention span of the pupils is not so much, as to attentively listen to the lecture extending from 40 to 50 minutes.

8. Useful for High Classes. It does not work successfully in lower classes. It can be used more profitably in higher classes.

9. Efficient Lecturer. The success of this method depends upon lecturing efficiency of the teacher. If this is not efficient, then he can never teach effectively.

10. Teaching becomes Dull. It makes teaching activity dull and uninteresting. The teaching-learning process becomes one way.

Precautions in Using the Lecture Method

While employing this method, the teacher should bear the following points in mind.

1. Proper Planning. Before delivering a lecture, the subject-matter should be properly planned. The lecture can never be successful unless the subject-matter is planned. He should have the ability to satisfactorily answer all types of questions, raised in the class.

2. Synopsis of the Lecture. Before lecturing he should prepare its synopsis or outline. This will facilitate in learning the main points.

3. Capable Teacher. As far as possible, teachers should develop lecturing ability. He should be a good speaker. He should be such as to modify his pronunciation, facial expressions etc. according to the topic.

4. Other Suggestions:

(a) Should try to lecture in the form of a free talk.

(b) Background and introduction should be prepared.

(c) While lecturing, he should note the facial expression of pupils, it will tell him, if the pupils are understanding or not.

(d) Should speak steadily and in a composed way. In between let there be pauses.

(e) He should pay particular attention to his pronunciation, language, style, defacial expression.

(f) In between teacher should ask questions and it will keep pupils attentive, and hert in the course of the lecture.

(g) There should be no tension. It should not be dry.

(h) At relevant places, teacher should take the help of examples, anecdotes etc.

(i) Due place should be assigned for evaluation under lecture method.

Project Method. No method has evoked mare interest than the Project Method. The term project in education came in use during, the early years .of this century and is a modern contribution to educational theory and practice. It is the outcome of philosophy of education and is a natural extension of the problem method. But the credit of unit acting this method goes to Professor *William Kilpatrick,* who has defined it as "a whole-hearted purposeful activity, proceeding in a social environment." *Dr. J.A. Stevenson* who perfected it as a method of teaching. According to him, "A project is a problematic act carried to completing in its natural setting." It is, in fact, that, form of coordinated activity which is directed towards the learning of a significant skill or process. It also involves the acquisition of useful information and also affects attitudes and interests.

Dr. W.H. Kilpatrick of Columbia University defined Project as "Whole hearted purposeful activity proceeding in a social environment". *J.A. Stevenson* gave a definition that relates to the teaching of Agriculture of the early years. He states that a project is it problematic at carried to completion in its natural setting. He has not been able to explain as to what constitutes a natural setting in the educational process. Billard defines, "A project is a bit of rear life that has been imparted into the school."

From the point of view of Commerce, the term should be restricted to a pupil-planned, purposeful task, accomplished in a real life like situation. It is a reaction against dull, mountainous, purposeless and lifeless class-room teaching.

Basic Principles of the Project Method

Project method is based on the following principles:

1. The Principle of Purpose. Effective learning is possible only when the child is interested in purpose full earning and for this:

(a) The school work should be related to child's outside life and

(b) The child should realise that he can achieve some purpose or objective in pursuing that work.. Only then they will put their life and soul in the educational task. They take little interest in an activity which is aimless or which is not purposeful or which does not combine life with learning. The success of any project is largely determined by the degree to which the pupils identify themselves with it and adopt it as their own.

2. The Principle of Activity. Mere securing interest of the child is not sufficient. Because every child is active by nature and physical and mental experiences derived from activity are more educative and retentive. A child should be given ample opportunities—for working on things, projects and these should be profitably exploited for education.

3. The Principle of Experience. Physical and mental activities provide experience and should be such as are useful to the children for educational purposes. When a child works in groups he learns to cooperate with others and thus share their interests and purposes. He gets valuable social experiences in cooperative living, character building and practical democracy and citisenship.

4. The Principle of Reality. Children should be provided with those activities which look like real life situations. If education is a preparation for life, the school must create real life situations in the school premises. They should be made to learn to solve actually life situations and problems. Because life itself is full of projects and problems.

5. The Principle of Freedom. The desire to learn should grow out of pupil's own needs and purposes. The desire for any activity should be spontaneous and not forced by the teacher. The project should grow out of the child's own interests and purposes and a child should be free to plan and do things. There should be no fixed time-table and no rigid curriculum. The children should be left to themselves in an atmosphere of freedom—freedom to choose the activity according to their capacities and mental power. There should be no impositions and restrictions.

6. The Principle of Utility. The knowledge gained through any educational activity must be useful and practical. Doing various activities alone is not important. Their importance lies in their practical utility. Project ensures this because activity is done in actual life-situations and achieves best educational results.

Procedure of a Project

There are different steps in the project though these may not be clearly visible in all cases but they are there in all projects. Every project has six steps.

1. Providing a Situation for the Selection of the Project. The teacher of Commerce should first know the interest and aptitude of the students and then he is to provide them a situation involving a problem affecting society. He is to leave the students to examine, observe and study the problem from all aspects and realise the necessity and importance of solving it. The teacher's job is to provide such a situation according to the pupil's interest and aptitude as may give them spontaneous urge to carry out a project. Situations caliber created by conversation, discussion, pictures, stories, visits and excursion, etc. Students may then be prompted to choose the project after having examined several situations. When the children make unsuitable choice, the teacher should direct and guide, them and explain to them the difficulties and undesirability of the project selected by them and to persuade them to take up some other suitable project.

2. Judging the Project. This is a stage, where the students review their work and try to find out what mistakes they have made in planning or in carrying out the project. It is a sort of self-criticism which is a very important form of training and should never be neglected.

3. Purposing. This is a very important step in a project. "The most important thing about it is that the pupils do the purposing". There is a tendency on the part of some teachers to choose the project for their students and making them to accept the choice but such an effort has very little educative value. If the project has been proposed by them they will be able to plan and carry out in a better way.

4. Planning and Executing the Project. Under the able and expert guidance of the teacher the students will plan out the project. The teacher has to the students the necessity of planning. For this purpose oral discussions should be held among the students for execution, the teacher should assign the work to students according to their ability and interest.

5. Self-criticism-evaluation. Self-criticism includes the choice of the project, its planning, duties assigned to right type of students, difficulties felt. How to avoid these mistakes in future and how to improve them in future? They learn to criticise their own work. Whether or not the aim was achieved? Whether the goal set was achieved? The evaluation of the project should be made, in the first instance, by the pupils and afterwards by the teacher.

6. Recording of the Work Done. The children record their findings in their note-books. They should put down a complete record of all the activities connected with the project.

Text-Book Method. Defined as "that teaching procedure in which the mastery of the text-book is the immediate objective." Text-book method means the procedure which "revolves around the text-book just as another procedure might revolve around the problem or the project". However, we may find good as well as bad teaching within the limits of the text-book method.

While text-book is a very useful means of getting incise and up-to-date information, an oral lesson may become lengthy, complicated and unintelligible. A text-book is logically and systematically arranges the subject-matter for students.

If the teacher bases all of his leaching upon a single text-book, the text-book procedure may become undesirable. As generally followed in schools in this procedure the teacher or one of the students, reads the text-book in the class. The teacher explains difficult words and sentences and removes flaws in reading and pronunciation. Text-book is not an end in itself but only a means. A text-book is an effective aid and must be taken as such. One text-book should never be completely depended upon. To supplement the subject-matter given in one particular text-book other text-books, references and resources should also be consulted.

Advantages of Text-Book in Commerce

1. Meeting the Need of the Students. From the students point of view, a text-book should meet their requirements by the use of simple language, headings, sub-headings, questions, assignments, maps, charts, pictures and other illustrative material.

2. Developing Study Skills. Provides a common basis on which the process of reading, analysing outlining and summarising can be mastered. A text-book furnishes a common laboratory in which study skills can be developed. By studying the text-book independently at home and understanding its content the student develops study skills.

3. Suggesting Application of the Material. A text-book suggests application of the subject-matter, through assignments, drills, questions, projects and other activities in commerce.

4. Reflecting and Establishing Standards. A text-book indicates what the teacher is required to teach and what the pupils are supposed to learn in commerce. By its teaching and learning aids, text-book greatly affects methods and establishes the standards of scholarship. It furnishes a definite basis for specific assignments, problems, and projects. Through it the teacher can easily establish class as well as individual standards.

5. Expanding and Limiting its Scope and Sise, According to Needs. According to the changing needs of education a textbook can expand and delimit its scope, sise and content. Sometimes it leads and sometimes follows the educational process.

6. Giving an Accurate Account of the Subject. A text-book is very useful as it gives a reasonably correct logical and systematic account of the subject field in an organised manner.

7. Presenting Different and Opposing Points of View on Historical and Current Events. A text-book presents history and current affairs in such a way as to develop in pupils an appreciation of different points of view.

8. Presenting Content, Relating to Human Relationship. Giving an accurate account of our environment, the values and principles which guide our actions and the processes through which we hope to improve ourselves. A social studies text-book helps in improving the physical and mental well-being of our pupils.

9. Basis of Almost all Other Methods. As all post all other methods can be used with the text-books as a basis of study assignment procedure or telling and discussion method or even problem, project and unit methods can be used with advantage with the help of a text-book.

Limitations of the Text-Book

1. Rote Memorisation. Students generally memories text-book word for word and reproduce the same in black and white at the time of examination. Accepting blindly what is given in the text-book they feel that it contains all the needed information and knowledge. However, enriched scholarship of the teacher can be a suitably guarantees against this limitation.

2. Contains only Minimum Essential. Containing only a summary treatment of the subject-matter a text-book does not give lively details. It, thus, leaves a lot to be done by the teacher. Without teacher's planning and direction the students cannot derive full advantage of the text-book.

3. Possibility of Errors of Detail and Interpretation. There is a possibility of errors of detail and interpretation as the whole field of subject-matter in a text-book is to be condensed and encompassed by an author to meet the requirements of students. This defect can be removed if the teacher is competent enough to correct errors and counteract prejudiced interpretations.

4. Tendency to Dominate. Because of its definite and convenient subject-matter a text-book may dominate the entire procedure of teaching. Covering a certain number of pages the students and teachers may drift into the habit of routine procedure accepting anything that they see in print. This limitation can also be overcome by the utilisation of other aids.

Thus, too much reliance should not be placed upon the text-book. The text-book method is not a complete method in itself. The teacher should make to liberalise the lecture method and the supplementary references, maps, charts, pictures and other aids and materials to supplement text-book. In classes where a single text-book is used the pupils should be encouraged to make use of a variety of supplementary materials, according to their interests and abilities. Challenging assignments should be given to meet their individual differences and to facilitate their learning, so as to motivate the pupil for self-activity in learning.

6

Audio-Visual Aids

In Commerce, various modern methods are there to impart all kinds of experiences, and explain and expand ideas. That is why, in order to organise and to impart full knowledge it becomes necessary to use pictures, maps, graphs and charts, etc. which represent social facts. Their use, not only helps in pupils learning, but they come to know also those things which are necessary in daily life. Through their effective use, pupils get a lot of help in understanding current events, 'Because of their use, the child is conscious every moment, to receive new ideas and under such new-situations, he acts intelligently. In Commerce, great need is self for the development of concepts, improvement of attitudes and expansion of interests. Due to their use, pupils can properly hear lessons taught in the class, and hence become the basis for group planning, logical deliberation and collective exchange of views.

Importance. In the words of *E.B.Weslley*, "All audio-visual aids provide experiences. Through their use relations between words and objects are easily established. Pupils save time and with their help they come to know about simple and correct facts." These, on the one hand, amuse pupils, and on the other, pupils learn to appreciate various things. Complicated things become simple. These develop imagination power of pupils and their observation. Quite possible, that a need may arise to define such an arrangement but, it needs no translator, since in these the universal language of nature, colour, condition, pace is employed. Thus, they offer royal road far learning.

1. Senses are Gate-ways of Knowledge. Senses are considered as the gate-ways for learning. So, the experiences acquired through senses, facilitate learning. The child cannot understand new wards and unfamiliar things, till these are related to his experiences. Audio-visual aids help greatly in acquiring experiences related to senses. Small children particularly need concrete experiences. In Commerce, direct and indirect, both types of experiences are important for which audio-visual aids prove helpful.

2. Clarity and Reality in the Learning Situation. These aids are quite interesting and inspiring. These bring clarity and concretness in the learning of the topic. These are good means of attracting and focussing attention and arousing interests on the part of the pupils.

3. Help in Stimulating the Process of Learning. These not only accelerate learning, but they do not forget these experiences for quite long time, because of these aids pupils become curious and begin to take active part in learning process.

4. Useful for Slow Learners. These aids greatly help the slow learners. Such children cannot comprehend all essential things from the text-books and so they are considered backward. Such children can easily learn and assimilate new things with the help of pictures, films, models, radio etc.

5. Helpful in Imparting Direct Experiences. These are complementary to direct experiences. While teaching about life in the past of the remote regions, it may not be quite possible to give them direct experience. On such occasions these aids can greatly help in understanding new concepts, facts and symbols and in place of direct experiences we can very effectively use pictures, models etc. Sometimes the use of silent or talking films saves a lot of time and as compared with the knowledge directly gained, much more knowledge is acquired, in this way.

6. Help in Stimulating Imagination and Thinking. The aids which impart perceptual knowledge are for more effective and explicit than the original ones. So, with their use, teaching process becomes natural and simple. The audio-visual aids stir imaginative capabilities and also develop observation, analytical and synthetical abilities. Thus aids can be highly useful in this direction.

7. Helpful to Attain Perfect Knowledge. It has been experimental proved that the pupils, through the proper use of aids, not only quickly learn, but they retain for longer time whatever is learnt. When pupils see, hear, touch, taste, smell, their experiences get concretised and those become stable to a considerable extent. Knowledge got with the help of pictures, models, charts or by similar aids, can be recalled at proper time. So, we can say that knowledge acquired through the use of the aids, becomes strengthened.

8. Opportunities for Activities. Through the use of these aids, pupils get opportunities for doing various kinds of activities. Pupils get opportunities for discussion, after a film is shown.

9. Meets Shortage of Resources. Their use removes the deficiencies of those are as of school and thereby compensates the scarcity of subject experts. For example, radio lessons by good teachers and the T.V., telecast of lessons of Commerce are there.

10. Develop Scientific Attitude. The use of A.V aids in the class, with the systematic use of other material based on technological principles, develops scientific outlook in pupils.

In the end, the need and importance of these aids lies in creating a teaching-learning situation by putting the teacher and pupils in an environment full of life, activity, casting permanent impact. In this way, at all levels of teachers training the training in the use of audio-visual aids is important.

Types of Teaching Aids

Basing his classification upon the kinds of experiences presented through the aids *Edgar Dale* calls it the "Cone of Experience." As classified by him, the range of experience through audio-visual aids is between direct experience and pure abstraction. These division overlap and sometimes blend into each other. Dale desires the cone of experience to be a 'visual metaphor' of learning experiences depicting the various

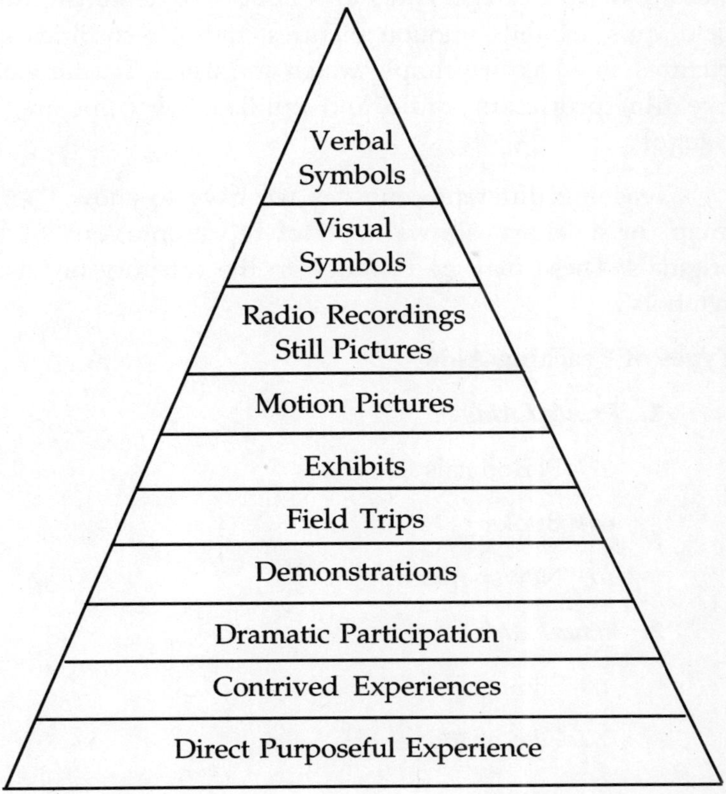

Cone of Experience

items in the order of increasing abstractions as one proceeds from direct purposeful experience which is the bedrock of all education. At the second stage are used the contrivances like models.

Dramatics invoke a reconstructed experience and step in where contrivances fail. Participation is better than mere watching.

As generally we cannot participate in the experience and have to be spectators. Observation, comes upper-most in education. This category includes items like demonstrations, field trips, exhibits, motion pictures, radio, recordings and pictures, in which we simply watch and listen. Teaching aids like film projectors, radio and epidiascope come in this category.

Teaching different countries we have to show them a 'map' or a 'chart' shows abstract representations of the originals. These may be included in the category of 'visual symbols'.

Types of Teaching Aids

1. ***Printed Aids***

   (i) Periodicals

   (ii) Books

   (iii) Newspapers

2. ***Visual Aids***

   (i) Slides

   (ii) Film strips

   (iii) Models

   (iv) Graphs and Charts

(v) Pictorial materials

(vi) Globes and Maps

3. ***Audio Aids***

(i) Tape Recordings

(ii) Phonograph discs

(iii) Radio

4. ***Audio-Visual Aids***

(i) Motion Pictures

(ii) Television

(iii) Dramatisation.

What is an Audio-Visual Aid?

Audio-Visual Aids have been defined in these words: "Any device which by sight or sound increases the individual's experience, beyond that acquired through reading, may be described as an audio-visual aid to learning." It is only a means of stimulating interest at a particular time, during the course of a lesson. Audio-Visual aids are additional means to particular ends and at times contribute valuable aids to learning a situation. They arouse curiosity and interest about the extension, application and development of the topic in hand. They provoke additional mental activity. They satisfy a felt need and enrich or improve the child's understanding about a particular topic for which it has been utilised. They must be used in full context to some point in the lesson and not for the sake of entertainment aids used merely, for their entertainment value, contribute nothing to learning. These cannot be considered as teaching aids.

Advantages of Audio-Visual Aids

According to *Edgar Bruce Weslley*, audio-visual aids furnish experiences. They facilitate the association of objects and words. They save pupil's time and they provide simple and authentic information. They enrich and extend one's appreciation and furnish pleasant entertainment They provide a simplified view of complicated data. They stimulate the imagination and develop the pupil's power of observation. These aids may need explanation but they do not need translators. They speak a universal language of form, colour, position and motion. They constitute one of the royal roads to learning. Following are the advantages of these aids:

1. **Provision of Sensory Experience.** Learning requires an adequate background of sensory experience. New words and unfamiliar objects cannot be followed and understood properly unless they are attached to specific, elements of one's experience. However, both direct and indirect learning experiences are important in the teaching of Commerce. Lessons should have a multiple sense appeal as stimuli, which appeal to more than one sense organ, are perceived and remembered easier and better.

2. **Supplement to Direct Experience.** Direct experiences can very well be supplemented with audio-visual aids by vicarious or representative learning visiting a post office or a cotton textile mill pupils can learn more about the postal system and about the manufacture of cloth if these direct learning experiences or followed by seeing a film or motion picture on the subject. Seeing such a film adds to the information already gained from actual visits and trips.

3. **Important Motivators.** Audio-visual aids are important motivators. They possess vividness, clarity and dramatic appeal. Children enjoy looking at pictures, going to movies and listening to the radio. These are effective medium of holding the attention

and to stimulating new interests and activities among children. These motivate pupils to learn faster, remember longer, gain more accurate information and understand the delicate concepts and meanings better. Aids motivate learning as they satisfy the immediate curiosity of the child.

4. **Provision of Substitutes for Direct Experiences.** Audio-visual materials will come to our aid all that time to facilitate the understanding of new concepts, facts and symbols. Pictures, models and specimens etc. may be used as accurate and effective substitutes of direct learning experiences. At times the study of particular films and still pictures may be more economical saving a lot of energy and time and giving us even more knowledge of the facts or objects that is possible through direct learning experiences.

5. **More Efficient Learning.** With the proper use of audio-visual aids pupils not only learn more rapidly but they also remember the facts, thus learned, for longer period. As a child sees, hears, touches, tastes and smells, his experiences are more permanent. As mental images created by pictures, models, charts and other such aids are easy to recall more efficient learning is possible.

6. **Meaningful Learning.** Verbal descriptions of abstract things are beyond the comprehension of young children. Meaningful material is easily learned and assimilated by the child and forgotten at a slower speed. Learning involves knowledge as well as meaning of things. Rich meaning provides rich learning. Audio-visual aids break the monotony of the formal type of teaching, and provide meaning to each and everything used or displayed in the class.

7. **Effective Aid to the Slow Learner.** Audio-visual aids are particularly helpful to poor readers and slow-learners who cannot get all the required knowledge from the text-book. They can more easily understand and remember the facts, gained through pictures, movies, models and radio etc. than gathered from abstract symbols and printed pages.

8. **Development of the Power of Imagination and Observation.** Audio-visual aids provide sensory images much more clear and effective than the verbal images. It makes learning more natural and easy. Audio-visual aids stimulate imagination and develop the power of observation, analysis and synthesis.

Correct Use of the Audio-Visual Aids

1. Use when Required. Audio-visual aids should be used when and where necessary. These are not to be used just for the sake of using.

2. Simple. The audio-visual aids should be simple creating only genuine interest and arousing too much of curiosity, because, otherwise their pupils' attention will be distracted and they will pay attention to the aids rather than to the lesson.

3. Treat as Means. The teacher must treat audio-visual aids as the means to an end.

4. Preferably Grow before the Students. Generally speaking, there are occasions when it is better to draw a map, a sketch, a diagram or a graph on the black-board in front of the students.

5. Properly Exhibited. In proper exhibition a number of factors should be kept in mind for example, the teacher should not place a number of audio-visual aids before, the students. He should keep them hidden and bring out only that aid when it is required to be shown. He should see before hand that there is nail etc., on the wall to hang the picture or the chart. He should see that the, apparatus works properly. The audio-visual aids should be exhibited before the students for a sufficiently long time, so that their curiosity is satisfied, and they have properly observed what is required to be observed.

Audio-Visual Aids

Followings are the aids of Audio-Visual used in schools:

Black-Board/Chalk-Board

To teach with the help of black board/chalk board is one of the oldest methods. Now in place of black board, chalk boards are being used. These, instead, of being black, may be green, yellow or of any of colour. Commerce/Science teachers have started experiencing that chalk board can be very useful for them. Their use can be made for various points along with framing outline of any topic for drawing and sketching diagrams, figures, plans to develop and to write summary. Since black board is the cheapest and easily available, its proper utilisation can render wonderful help in teaching Commerce. Many teachers feel that they cannot properly write on black board. But let it be mentioned here that this skill is necessary for every teacher whether he teaches Commerce, or Language, Maths, Science or any other subject. It is true that for teaching Commerce many types of charts, graphs, outlines are available in the market. But it cannot be denied that the best ones are those which are prepared in the presence of pupils. The chart or the map that is drawn in the presence of the pupils is formable beneficial than the one already drawn before hand. That is why ability to draw a sketch or a good picture on the black board by the teacher is so much important. Do not crowd the aids at anyone time. To emphasise different points, ideas and concepts pieces of chalk of different colours be used and the work to be done should be planned in advance.

Importance of Black-Board/Chalk-Board

If it is used properly it become highly inspirational. It helps the pupils a lot to grasp the write-up. While teaching a lesson, any picture displayed, can draw the attention of the class. By writing on the black-board of drawing sketches, the teacher can emphasise the main points. Using lines, he can draw and present to the class, a map or a picture. Black-board is a means which is ever present in the class. For its use neither technical knowledge nor the skill of high artistic nature is required.

Use of Black-Board/Chalk-Board

In teaching of Commerce the use of the black-board/ chalk-board can be made as follows:

1. To write summary
2. To explain the relationship and importance of a name or a term
3. To write outlines of a plan
4. To present chart, line drawing, graph or symbolic representation
5. To give main instruction
6. To explain the sequence of a thing
7. To write rules and definition
8. To give information relating to dates, table, statistics etc.

Important Facts Relating to the Use of Black-Board

The Commerce teacher, while using the black-board, should keep the following in mind:

1. Before starting the class-work collect all necessary things; duster, chalk, scale, stencils, protector etc.

2. Rub off the Black-Board with the duster, and not by fingers.

3. Start writing on it from the left hand top corner. Write only important points on it. Remember that it is not suitable for extensive work.

4. Use a pointer to focus attention of the pupils on the map or drawing sketched on it.

5. Plan in advance what to write on it. Do not draw/ display any map before hand or take help of any book continuously.

6. Write neatly and uniformly on it. In addition whatever may be written on it, should be in a serial order, so that pupils develop habit to write in a sequence.

7. It should be located at a place so as to be visible to all pupils with facility. Let there be no reflection of light on it. It should not be at a greater height of the vision level of the pupils, and the desks in the front row should be at least eight feet away from the black board.

8. The letters written on it, should be bold so that pupils may easily see them. Words in small sise should not be written on it. What ever be written on it, should be in straight lines.

9. While writing on it, teacher should not cover it, but standing at the angle of 45°, he should write on it. If he does not do that, chances of indiscipline will arise in the class.

10. It should be repainted at least once a year.

11. While writing on it, at times, the teacher should cast a glance at pupils.

12. After writing on it, he should stand on one side of the black-board. He should surprise the class and attend to individual difficulties of pupils. He should do this so that each pupil can see every-thing written on it.

13. As he writes on it, he should speak out the same simultaneously.

The conclusion is that the black-board/chalk-board is an important aid in teaching this subject.

Visual Aids

1. Real Objects. If during teaching, real objects are used as teaching aids, their impact will be far greater than that of all other types of aids. If the parts of the plots are to be taught, then the lesson may be taught with the help of the real plant. This will create in pupil a sense of joy and interest. So, as far as possible, real objects alone be used as teaching aids, like bones, feathers of the bird, specimens of claws, butterflies, leaves, flower, metalic coins, specimens of rocks, machine and tools, tickets etc. To stock them is the best course. Specimen of different types of corn can be stored in small bottles. Put the flower or leaf on the blotting paper and press the same tinder a heavy book and in four to five days, it will take flat shape. Preserve it in a file. Fine and scarce objects may be displayed, putting them in glass containers or almirahs.

2. Diagrams. To explain an object, fully, a diagram is drawn with the lines. To give clear and proper knowledge in science and geography teachers use diagrams. In drawing diagrams no expenditure is incurred and no special duration of time is required.

(i) Diagram drawn on the black board then and there has a lasting impact on the children.

(ii) To explain, plants and flowers in Botany and display of different parts of human body, in life science, the diagrams can be drawn on the black-board.

(iii) While showing the diagrams, real objects or film strips and pictures can also be shown. That will have more lasting impact. Diagrams should be simple so that those can be easily understood. Diagrams should be suitable to the topic. In order to explain the meaning, the teacher may use coloured pieces of chalk, from time to time to make diagrams attractive.

All topics of the syllabus and all kinds of subject-matter, can be expressed with the help of diagrams as visual aids. But the success of this depends upon the fact that the diagrams and symbols be made the medium of expression which can be fully grasped by the pupils and the meaning of which they can understand properly. For example, the diagrams displaying the internal structure of the power, of the ear or of the eye along with the functioning cannot be properly explained unless the pupils thoroughly know in advance the symbols used in the diagrams. Hence the diagrams do not render any help in so far as the teaching of the subject-matter in the initial stage is concerned. In subsequent stage, that is of presentation or of study or of recapitulation, the diagrams can play an important role.

3. Chart. It is visual aid through which pupils can be acquainted with clear pictures of the subject-matter. The use of charts, enhances learning process. The use of charts can be done easily and effectivity in all subjects. They are available readmade in the market. If these are not available in the market, then the teacher himself can prepare them suitable to the lesson. The figures in the charts must be big enough so that the pupils sitting in all corners can be benefited. Small figures kill the interest of the pupil and they have to face inconvenience. There is a fear of indiscipline in the class. The picture drawn on the chart must be clear and definite.

Charts are of various types. The teacher may get charts prepared relevant to the topic and can use the same as a teaching devices. Some of them are as under:

(i) ***Time Chart.*** It can be called the time table. These are presented mostly, in accordance with historical/ chronological events, period, different rulers and battles. These show the time span of events and develop time sense.

(ii) ***Table Chart.*** In these charts heads are drawn under which events/accounts are given. These give the serial order of historical events, of rulers, of wars and the list of the same, according to time.

(iii) ***Picture Chart.*** Various pictures are collected and shown in the chart *i.e.,* means of transport, means of irrigation, postal agencies etc.

(iv) ***Flow Chart.*** In these charts the sequential growth of an object can be shown or the rise and fall of the monarchs can also be shown. Charts can also be made of the structure and development of law.

(v) ***Tree Chart.*** It can show the gradual development of a thing. The trunk of the tree is the main form and the branches show the development. Best examples are in botany, regarding the development of plants of insects in zoology. Just as branches and leaves sprout from the trunk, the chart develops in the same way.

(vi) ***Graph Chart.*** Such charts are used in teaching geography and Commerce, these are used to display statistical figures *e.g.,* rainfall and temperature, rainfall and population growth etc. These are of five kinds—area, picture, line, length, graph etc.

(vii) Pictorial Chart. That which displays small picture *e.g.*, rice bag, wheat sacks, animal pictures.

4. Posters. Posters have special importance in teaching of Commerce/Science. In a way, posters are the pictures of things, persons, places and events but in them the pictorial expression, as of the pictures, is not quite clear and in a direct way but with a special angle and indirect and symbolic form. General pictures can present entire description of the subject-matter. Through poster, one idea is made the point of focus and a forceful emotional appeal is made, whichever special message or a particular fact is supposed to inspire the pupils, and it fully captures their mind and heart that is why, in the world of advertisement and publicity its help is taken to the extent of which no other material is put through posters. Due to their different style these create an imposing environment so as to change or modify a trend or to inspire an action by which the role is played not only for bringing about desirable modifications in the behaviour of the individual only but also to turn the masses in the desired direction and full help can be got in propagating specific plans and movements.

To convey a message to pupils in an attractive manner, instruction given through posters is considered to be good. Posters can be on any subject, so as to cast influence on the pupils. Attractive posters have few words. The picture, cartoon or a diagram are presented in a fine way, so that pupils catch the message quickly. The thought in the posters should be clear and the same should be set in a chain so that the feeling could be caught. The choice of colours and contrasts should be appropriate. The writing on the poster should be big in sise so that pupils can see the same vividly. With the help of these posters, the teacher leaves a lasting impact on the children, about teeth, ear, eyes, washing of clothes, harm done by eating polluted stuff, importance of cleanliness etc. Posters can be prepared with the help of cuttings and clippings, magazine, pictures etc. Posters are prepared on paper, wood, cloth and plywood in different colours. They can be of any sise. So, the sources for getting posters by the teacher are put under two groups, the external and internal. Outside the school whatever can be obtained from the advertising and publicity agencies of the community, and suitable selection can be made out of the same. The teacher with the help of the pupils, and under his personal influence, should try to stock them. In the form of personal source also, the school, using the creative talents of the pupils, should try to prepare posters. In their preparation, collection and use, the following things should be borne in mind.

(i) The educational utility of the posters must be given more importance and only those posters should be collected or prepared which can help achieve specific instructional objectives.

(ii) The class teacher should use only those posters which help the pupils to understand properly, and which can play forceful role in bringing about expected modification in their behaviour.

(iii) The class teacher should select and use posters keeping in mind the proportion relating to clarity, simplification, attractive force, and to focus thoughts and stir emotion.

Bulletin Board

For both the teacher and the student the bulletin board is a sheet of wood, masonite, cork, celetex, or similar material set within a frame. Used for displaying pictures, charts, posters, clippings, photographs, or other learning materials, it serves as a perpetual magazine for the students of commerce. It gives information of direct concern to the pupils and tap their curiosity and desire for knowledge. It provides a practical outlet for artistic talent and creative ability. It helps to unify class spirit by creating a sense of responsibility, appreciation an accomplishment. It stimulates student's interest and enthusiasm for, a particular lesson. The bulletin board must be simple. It should telegraph its message quickly, easily and efficiently. The materials must be changed frequently. Tendency to overload the bulletin board must be resisted. Display must be done neatly and well.

Possibilities of Use

Unlimited possibilities of use exist for effective bulletin board displays. These might depict any number of themes such as agriculture through the ages, media of communication, political parties in the country, elections, food, fads and fallacies, etc. These use such materials as cartoons, newspapers, book jackets, ribbons or coloured strings, posters, snap shots, etc. Displays can be developed to illustrate local history, industrial achievements, famous personalities, foreign lands and people, various products, etc. Maps, drawings, graphs and pictures may be combined to present facts, stir the imagination and call for action on anyone of these themes.

Displays on the bulletin board should be attractive, appropriate, meaningful, timely and interesting. These may include pictures, posters pamphlets, cartoons, graphs, maps, charts, diagrams, news-items, feature articles, magazine articles and samples of pupil's creative work. A judicious selection of such displays should be made after critical inspection and approval by teacher or the committee appointed for this purpose. Each display should be a unit, containing one central theme.

Suggestions to Use the Bulletin Board Effectively

1. Display interesting and understandable material on the bulletin board.

2. Rebate the material should, to the topics being studied in the class.
3. Make balanced and artistic arrangements with appropriate headings, titles, explanatory notes, mountings and colours etc., to make the display meaningful.
4. Change the material according to purposes and problems.
5. Give ample opportunities to the pupils to explore to and discuss the material displayed or to be displayed on the bulletin board.
6. Give the pupils opportunities to assist in arranging and re-arranging materials, which they have prepared or brought from home, for display.

7

Importance of Text-Book

Teacher may use any of the methods of teaching he feels a necessity of text-books. The work of the teacher does not end in the classroom he has to see that the pupil can readily apply the knowledge gained by him in the classroom. For this it is desirable to provide the student with a record of class-work and also some questions for practice. This record can be had, by the pupil, by taking notes in the class, but these lengthy dictation and notes may prove to be most-time consuming. A good text-book saves the times of the teacher as well as of the taught.

A text-book is probably the cheapest and most reliable source of information. It also serves as a reference book for the teacher the students to acquire the required information with speed. While revising his lessons a pupils can work independently making use of text-books at his disposal. A text-book helps this students in thoroughly understanding the subject-matter. It also helps the students to make up his deficiency because of his failure to attend certain classes due to unavoidable reasons.

A teacher can make use of the text-book to give home-work and assignments to the pupils. The text-book specifies the standards expected to be attained by a particular class. It also gives suggestion about the use of various teaching aids and activities to be undertaken. A text-book also helps the teachers In teaching and correlating the subject with other things. It lays down the order of procedure.

In lower classes text-books with colored illustrations provide an incentive to learning and they provide attraction for the young learner. That is why a text-book for every child has become an essential equipment.

How to use a Text-Book?

A text-book is valuable only if it is used properly. The teacher should not consider that his work is confined to transferring the contents of the text-book into the heads of the pupils. The text-book should not be used as the only source of instructional material. It should be used as an aid in teaching not a substitute for teaching. It is a means and not an end in itself. Its place in teaching can only then be real if the teacher supplements is by his oral exposition, by reference reading and by all his illustrating and objective techniques. It should be followed carefully and intelligently and not slavishly.

For an average teacher the text-book is all his stock-in-trade. The greater the capacity, knowledge, professional training and experience of the teacher, the less he needs to depend on his text-books, However, no teacher can afford to work entirely without a text-book. It is not a master to be feared, it is rather a servant to be ordered.

The contribution of the text-book can be increased by creating situations where the pupils have a real purpose for turning to the textbook. Assignment Method, Dalton Plan and Project work provide a larger scope for creating such situations.

Essentials of Good Text-Book

According to *Hall Quest,* "A good text-book" is

(i) a source of knowledge,

(ii) a guide,

(iii) a tool,

(iv) a means of interpreting truth, and

(v) an inspiration to the pupil.

At present there is a great need of good text-books in all the regional languages. But books are generally of low standard, excepting very few, due to apathetic attitude of authors, tendency to prefer quantity to quality, partiality in evaluating the text-books and so on.

Criterion of Good Text-Book

1. Author. The author should have a considerable experience of teaching the subject. The minimum academic and professional qualifications may also be prescribed for the author.

2. The Language and Structure. The text-book should be written in lucid, simple, precise and scientific language which is within the approach of an average students. Diagrams will add to the value of the book.

3. The Subject-Matter. A good text-book in home-science should deal with the subject matter in a systematic and orderly manner in psychological sequence. The standard should be gradually increased. The matter should create interest in the pupils and the variety of topic should correspond to the variety of interests which the pupils are expected to have.

4. Illustration. The pictures in a good text-book should be well drawn, realistic and coloured wherever necessary so that they make the learning very much convenient and quick. The pictures as far as possible should be proportionate in size, otherwise the information about them contained in the book is very likely to be misinterpreted.

Some times, too many details are stuffed into a small space with the result that no detail is clear to the young mind. The effort to save space results in loss of utility on the whole. Illustrations should be attractive and useful because they play a vital roll in raising the standard of a text-book. Therefore, it is correct to say, "One picture is worth a thousand words". For very young pupil they should be coloured and not in black and white.

5. Experience. A good text-book not only teaches, it also tests. For consolidation of learning, there should be new thought-provoking exercises followed by good summary. There should be problems graded in difficulty at the end of each chapter. In addition to this in a good textbook there should be a good index.

The exercises should not be merely of recaptulatory nature rather they should be such as to help to develop further concepts, desirable attitudes, technical skill and creative power. The exercises should offer further experience in developing the pupils power of thinking and reasoning.

6. Technical Considerations. For the physical appearance and set up of a good text-book due consideration be given to the following points.

(i) It should be printed on a good white paper.

(ii) The type used should be in accordance with the reading ability of the pupils, headings and sub-headings should be in still bolder types. The type-faces should be appropriate.

(iii) The building should be proper and strong to withstand rough use. It should not make the book-difficult to open. The cover page should be well designed and attractive.

(iv) The size of the text-book should be handy for the children for whom it is meant.

(v) There should be no mistake in printing.

(vi) The price should be reasonable which the majority of learners can easily afford to pay.

In addition to the above the following qualities are expected in a good text-book.

(i) It should be up-to-date in its subject-matter.

(ii) The symbols and terms used must be those which are popular. All new terms should be clearly and accurately defined.

(iii) It should offer detailed suggestions for correlation, project work, assignment work and field work.

(iv) There should be suggestion to improve study habits.

(v) There should not be any irrelevant matter.

(vi) It should facilitate the use of inductive, analytical heuristic and laboratory methods.

(vii) It should satisfy the demands of the examinations.

(viii) It should conform to the recommendations of various committees.

Criteria of a Good Text-book as Prescribed by the UNESCO Planning Mission

(i) It should first of all meet the requirements of the syllabus.

(ii) It should help in linking up the subject with the life practice. The pupils should be equipped with the "know how" of utilising the knowledge in everyday life.

(iii) The facts, concepts etc. should be modem and within the comprehension of the pupils.

(iv) The contents should contain only the established facts aiming at shaping integrated modern world out look. The content should be simple, brief, exact, definite and accessible.

Text-Book for Commerce Subjects

In contrast to arts subjects, commerce subjects are of practical utility. For these subjects we need very good text-books to serve to the needs of the teachers and the students. In commerce subjects we find a death of highly specialised and authoritative text-books. Because of these facts it becomes quite difficult to make a proper selection of a text-book in commerce subjects.

The following points may be kept in view while selecting a textbook in commerce subjects.

(i) **Attractiveness of Book.** It should be attractive.

(ii) **Name of the Book.** Its name should not be too technical and frightening. It should be such which is appealing, arouses interest of the students and indicates the nature of the subject matter.

(iii) **Author.** He should be an authority on the subject and must also be conversant with the methods of teaching of commerce subjects.

(iv) **Language.** It should be simple, flowing, easy, grammatically correct.

(v) **Date of Publication or Revision.** The book should be a recent publication and the year of publication must be mentioned on the text-book. In some subjects (*e.g.* Income Tax) old text-books may be out of date.

(vi) **Teaching Procedures Followed.** It should include variety of teaching procedures of business subjects.

(vii) **Nature of Content.** The text-book should include all the topics of the subject.

(viii) **Illustrations.** In a good text-book there should be sufficient illustrations such as pictures of peoples, things and places etc. The illustrations should be of reasonable size and should be related to text-book material. It is desirable that illustrations appear on the same side of the page, where principles have been discussed. They should have outlay captions and must be up-to-date.

(ix) **Kind of Questions and Number of Questions.** It should have question based on information, rules, principles, definitions and other data. The questions should be thought provoking and should deal with what, why and how? Some questions on application of rules etc. must be included. Such questions are of more importance in subjects such as Book-keeping, Arithmetic, Shorthand, Computer etc.

8

Teaching Competency in Commerce

In the words of *Tonne, Popham* and *Freeman,* "Much of the current education philosophy is based on the idea that the educative process is largely training in problem-solving".

The student is presented with a situation wherein he requires to learn, how to do a certain thing? In their way he realises a felt need and as a consequence learning takes place.

A teacher of skills subscribing to the above views might on the very first day in a type-writing class direct the discussion to the uses to be, derived from a course in type-writing, the student may take a decision to have a typed schedule pasted on a suitable place in his bed room so as to be school in time. In the class-room the teacher may then start the work with an exercise in tabulation or in short-hand, the students may be interested to write the names, of his friends, in short hand. In this way the class work will start with writing of any new word in which the student shows his interest.

There may be many a real life problems that may be presented to the students and he may be helped to solve it. In this way student may be motivated in the topic and may be helped to learn by problem solving.

Sub-conscious Learning of Basic Skills

The examples of sub-concious learning given by *Douglas, Blendford* and *Anderson*, "A teacher once had in a class a girl who was unusually expert in taking dictation on the stenotype. She quite often was hired to record discussion and proceedings at conventions and important Board meetings. She had the reputation of never missing a word in her recording, yet while she was recording, she habitually was reading, a book or magazine at the same time. She has developed her skill so highly that it was completely automised; her fingers reached instantly when the sound of the voice reached her ears. She had actually found that her records were more accurate when she deliberately kept her minds off her work."

Six Steps of Learning Skills

Dr. Khan opines, "There are six steps which are necessary to achieve mastery of the skill. They are pre-test, teach-test, the result, adopt the procedure, re-teach, re-test, and continue the process till the actual mastery is achieved". The use of there steps is essential to the skills teacher. The use of demonstration should be made in achieving mastery of skills. It is better for the teacher to demonstrate than to simply tell to the students. Demonstration is helpful because the student makes it a habit to practice the demonstrated technique. The effectiveness of the learning of skills can be checked by sufficiently practicing the skill. To achieve the stage of automatisation in any skill it should be practiced a number of times. The fingers of the typist should move at a fairly good speed when he types a letter from his short-hand notes this skill is developed only after several years of practice. To start with, he learnt type-writing from printed matter, then he learnt shorthand. With practice he learnt to write accurately, speedily and with perfection. Afterwards he must have learnt to type-write from his short-hand notes. With sufficient practice he has now reached a stage when he does not spell the words as they are typed, his eyes now see short-hand outlines that represent the words, sounds and phrases and he now correctly spells out every word. He inserts all the needed punctuations as a habit without any extra effort. Thus now he has reached a stage of automatisation.

Modern Pattern of Experts

The features of expert patterns as enunciated by *Tonne* are as follows:

(1) Establishment and maintenance of a steady, even flow of motion. All practice should be directed towards the acquisition of such a flow, even in the initial stage, at the expense of accuracy.

(2) Related performance unhampered by nervous tension and hurry.

(3) Easy and economical movements.

(4) Concentration upon the task at hand.

Teaching of Understanding and Application

To teach understanding and application is a very complex task and is much more difficult in comparison to teach mere facts and details. For teaching of understanding and application the teacher is required to be an expert on the subject and fully skilled in the subject. This type of teaching can be imparted by a process that would consist of understanding application and competency problem solving on the part of the teacher himself. The level of attainment of these factors is also different in teaching the important elements.

Expressing himself on this topic *Dr. Khan* opnies, "If the students understand any fact properly and are capable of applying the principle based on these facts, the problem is likely to be solved easily." A good office worker must develop such competencies which can help him in coping with the difficulties involved in performance of his job. For example, if he is an accountant, he should be able to prepare his books of accounts properly and he should have this understanding of the accounts so that in case there are any mistakes in recording he should be in a position to find out such mistakes with ease. The competencies of problem solving can be attained if understanding has been developed and capacity of applying learned principles has been attained.

Teaching of Competencies

It is agreed by all that the first step in the learning of Commerce Education is the learning of facts and skills. It is highly desirable for every one to be capable of application of the skill, understanding and attaining competency in solving the problem. Problem solving activity in the practical aspect of the skills learnt in any commerce subject. Let us take the example from accountancy. A successful accountant must be a practical person, should be able to record dealings properly and in a comprehensible manner so as to, be understandable to the Chief Executive or the employer, and the Government department.

In a similar way a company secretary should be fully capable of taking a dictation in short-hand and then type it out correctly, neatly and efficiently. She must also be capable of sending out the letter in good professional way.

Problem-Solving Process

Various steps of problem-solving process are as follows:

***(i)* To Determine the Problem.** For solving the problem it is essential to clearly outline and determine the problem. It would be desirable to have some significant and interesting problem.

***(ii)* To Fix the Limit of the Problem.** For every problem there are certain levels and limits. We have to tackle any problem only at the level of capability of the students and limits be fixed with this in view.

***(iii)* To Know the Existing Knowledge of the Students.** For fixing the limits of the problem in accordance with the level of the students attainment it is essential that the teacher knows about the existing knowledge of the students.

(iv) New Facts should be Acquired. It is essential to acquire some new facts which shall be needed for teaching activity and application of the skill.

(v) Problem Solutions should be Determined. There could be number of probable solutions to a problem. It is desirable to discuss the merits and demerits of all such possible problems and thus the best solution be determined.

(vi) Application of the Solution. The best solution having been determined it should then be applied to solve the problem.

Unit Method of Teaching

This is one of the methods of teaching generally used by teachers and is considered to be one of the best methods of teaching.

Alberty summarises the method as follows:

> "Unit teaching as it is being carried out at present involves: *(i)* board comprehensive problem, *(ii)* a series of related learnings for the entire group and individual learning in terms of specific needs, abilities or interests of students, *(iii)* a plan for evaluation of out comes. Usually Unit teaching involves three stages as follows:
>
> *(i)* The planning stage in which problems are clarified, alternate plans of work considered and decisions reached as to how the group shall proceed,

(ii) an extended working stage in which there is much group discussion library research, investigations, experimentation, individual and committee work, and the like, and

(iii) a culminating phase in which results are brought together, conclusions are reached and results are evaluated".

"It should be obvious that unit teaching is not only concerned with units of subject matter, but is equally concerned with a process of teaching which takes into account modem psychological principles of learning dealing with individual differences, goal sharing, pupil teacher planning and pupil self-evaluation. While these characteristics can not be claimed as the role property of the unit mathod. This method requires the inclusion of these characteristics in its plan and operation before true unit teaching can be achieved or clamied."

Dr. Khan gives a clarification of unit method in his book "*The Practice of Teaching in Secondary Schools*" by taking up the morrison plan. He writes as follows:

The morrison plan for teaching gave rise to unit teaching. "Much of the unit" teaching now found in high schools may be traced directly or indirectly to influence the *Morrison* Plan. Like *Herbert, Morrison* too had five teaching or learning steps in his plan. Various steps of Morrison Plan are as under:

(i) Exploration.

(ii) Presentation.

(iii) Assimilation.

(iv) Organisation

(v) Recitation.

Though the steps in *Herbert* Plan and *Morrison* Plan are similar, yet there are certain major distinctions between the two. Some of these distinctions are as follows:

(i) Herbert Steps were for a single recitation or class-room period where as *Morrison* Plan is to be used over several periods.

(ii) Herbertion steps can fit into any kind of learning but it was claimed by *Morrison* that attitudes of understanding, appreciation, special abilities and skills are quite different products of leraning and so they need different teaching techniques.

(iii) In Herbertian method learning is presented in fragments where as in *Morrison* Plan learning is taken as whole to be most effective.

9

Evaluation Principles in Commerce

The recent trends in learning and evaluation link them to behavioural objectives. According to a behaviourist psychology learning is defined as a change in the behaviour of an individual that can be described in terms of observable and measurable performance. The changes in behaviour are affected by providing experiences and thorough teaching. The test efficiency of teaching, to judge the progress of students and to discover their achievements and evaluate the whole school system, we require some sort of measuring tools. These tools are tests or examinations. Tests are essential to grade and rank pupils, however, if evaluation is used merely to indicate areas of study to which children have been exposed or for classifying and categorizing students, a great value is lost. The same loss occurs if evaluation is interpreted only as arriving at numerical or alphabetical ratings for report cards. In this way much of the positive use of evaluation as a means of teaching and learning could be destroyed.

Effective instructional planning and evaluation of students performance have always stressed on the statement of instructional objectives so that they are of great help to the student. According to *Muller,* an instructionally usable objective must state the intended outcome in terms of the terminal behaviour of students. Terminal behaviour here means the behaviour of students after the class-room instruction and evaluation is possible if the learning outcomes are carefully specified. By combining continuous evaluation with immediate application of what has been learned, the teacher can provide for.

(i) The stimulation of students who learn rapidly to greater growth toward goals by application of advanced works.

(ii) The identification of specific weaknesses and difficulties in functional understanding (concepts, principles, generalisation) and the needed reteaching of varied activities skills or problem solving abilities, and

(iii) The clarification, modification or complete alternation of the goals as needed for the unit.

Evaluation, teaching and learning are the three corners of the education system. Evaluation is concerned with finding out how far students have learned as a consequence of teaching. There are two kinds of evaluation depending upon whether the comparison of student is made with some absolute performance standard or with other students of a given group. These are known as criterion referenced evaluation and norm referenced evaluation.

Criterion-Referenced Evaluations

It assesses the students performance in terms of specified performance standard or criterion without any mention of the performance levels of the other students of the group. This evaluation method is related to mastery and developmental tests.

Norm-Referenced Evaluation

It assesses the students performance relative to other students of the group. Students are marks and relative ranks in this method of evaluation.

Purpose of Evaluation

Some of the purposes for which evaluation is needed can be summarised as follows:

(i) For determining the teaching-learning process.

(ii) For revision of curriculum.

(iii) For securing effective cooperation from the parents and the community.

(iv) To provide some objective basis for reporting progress of students.

(v) For determining the policies of promotion.

(vi) To provide guidance to pupils on the basis of their evaluation.

Thus we find that evaluation is an essential part of the educational process. It helps in realising the goals of instructions. It points out the defects in teaching learning process. It also helps 10 ascertaining the effectiveness of the curriculum, methods and devices of teaching etc.

Principles of Evaluation

In evaluation we reach a value judgment on the basis of the fixed principles of evaluation. In this connection the Secondary Education Commission opined, "The school of today concern. Itself not only with the intellectual pursuits but also with the emotional and social development of the child, his physical and mental health, his social adjustment and other equally important aspects of his life—is a word with all round development of his personality".

Evaluation is an attempt to know the extent of success of the child in various fields and to help him in making further progress. It is an attempt to measure the level of student's level of intelligence, attainment, aptitude and interest etc.

Our evaluation system should be such as to help us in understanding our pupils better so that he may be helped to overcome his difficulties.

These lays "Evaluation" is used for "Examinations". Evaluation has been defined by *Wrightston*, "Evaluation is a relatively new technical term introduced to design a more comprehensive concept of measurement implied in conventional tests and examinations". Examinations put more emphasis on measuring the students achievements in academic subjects only but in evaluation an attempt is made to measure all the changes that take place in the development of balanced personality and measure the qualities of head, hand, health and heart of the pupil.

Putting his opinion in respect of evaluation *M. Brown* writes, "Evaluation is essential in the never ending cycle of formulating goals measuring progress towards them and determining the new goals which emerge as a result of new warnings—evaluation involves measurement which means objective quantitative evidence. But it is broader than measurement and implies that considerations have been given to certain values, standards and then interpretation of the evidence has been made in the light of the particular situation."

In the opinion of *Good*, "Evaluation is a process of ascertaining of judging the amount of some thing by careful appraisal". From the above we can conclude that evaluation is concerned both with scholastic achievements and behavioural changes.

Guiding Principles of Evaluation

The principles of evaluation as suggested by Grim can be summarised as under:

(i) Evaluation takes into consideration the complete picture just as we consider the total personality of the child in learning.

(ii) For evaluation of the child an attempt is made to collect varied and relatively objective evidence.

(iii) Evaluation should enable the child to appraise himself.

(iv) Evaluation must be a continuous and cumulative process.

(v) For the success of evaluation process that teachers, parents, pupils, community, administration should participate in the process of evaluation.

(vi) Evaluation must be closely related to the guidance programme.

Devices of Evaluation in Commerce

There could be a number of devices of evaluation. Some of these are:

(i) Personality tests.

(ii) Essay type examinations.

(iii) Objective tests.

(iv) Interviews.

(v) Achievements tests.

(vi) Aptitude tests.

(vii) Check lists.

Evaluation in commerce which is a vocational subject, can be done according to the following framework:

(i) To determine and clarify what is to be evaluated.

(ii) Purpose of evauation.

(iii) An awareness of the limitation and strengths of various techniques used for evaluation.

(iv) Use of a variety of evaluation techniques.

(v) Evaluation is a means and not an end in itself, and

(vi) Evaluation of learning standards.

The following points are important to judge the effectiveness of commerce programme:

(i) Testing vocational skills on different standards of achievement.

(ii) Judging capacity of students.

(iii) Orienting them to new situations relating to commerce.

(iv) Testing the performance of students on some work, activity or employment.

(v) Examining students on basic concepts, principles or area of knowledge.

(vi) Making a rapport with inter-departmental coordination.

(vii) Broadening their knowledge of business and educational types.

(viii) Speed test and efficiency of skills.

(ix) Competitive performance in seminars, conferences and group discussion.

Planning of Tests in Commerce

For a proper planning of tests an expert knowledge and good deal of experience are required. A lot of time and energy are consumed in planning any good test. Before planning any good test the teacher should deliberate to fully understand the objectives to be assessed, the examines and their test-taking behaviour.

For planning a good test following steps are involved:

(i) Defining the population for which the test is to be conducted.

(ii) Defining the subject-matter for different subjects to be included in evaluation.

(iii) Defining the purpose of evaluation.

(iv) Analysing the objectives of evaluation.

(v) Determining relative emphasis to be put on various content areas and objectives.

(vi) Determining the types of items to be used.

(vii) Determining the level of difficulties of various items to be used.

(viii) Preparation of a blue print.

Characteristics of Good Test in Commerce

A good test in commerce should have the following characteristics:

***(i)* Validity.** The test should be valid. It should fulfil the objectives for which it is meant. If our aim is to measure the ability to understand and application of commercial facts then language difficulty and speed should not come in way. Thus it should be free from defects that are likely to affect the valid results.

***(ii)* Reliability.** Its test is considered to be reliable if it gives same results every times when it is used for testing the individuals abilities under same conditions. An objective test is bound to be reliable.

The reliability of a test is affected by the following factors, thus to be reliable it should be free from:

(a) The whims of an examiner.

(b) The physical and mental condition of the students.

(c) The language of the questions-lack of clearness or any ambiguities in statements.

(d) Lack of clear-cut instructions for marking.

(e) Inefficient methods of scoring.

A reliable test is not influenced by subjective conditions, it is objective.

***(iii)* Comprehensiveness.** Any good test should be comprehensive i.e. it should assess knowledge, skills, abilities, attitudes etc. as adequately as possible. No aspect of the curriculum should be ignored while making evaluatation.

***(iv)* Capable of Maintaining the Interest of the Students.** Any good test should be able to capture the interest of the students and maintain it. Thus it should be interesting for the students. A good test is motivating for the students and stimulates their best efforts. It should be neither too easy nor too difficult. It should never be used as a means of punishment.

***(v)* Administrability.** It should be easy to administer, economical in time and money, easy to score and interpret. The directions of the test should be clear-cut. There should be answer-keys for scoring.

***(vi)* Utility.** A good test is useful in various way. For example a test result may be used for improvement of teaching, may be useful to measure some desired quality/ability in the student, useful in finding out deficiencies in pupils so that remedial measures be taken up for their removal etc.

***(vii)* Diagnosticity.** A good test is diagnostic. The aim of diagnostic is to analyse the difficulties of a students in a particular phase of work. The aim is to reveal reliable information concerning his weakness in order to overcome them by concentrated action and for remedial teaching. In this way it would help the teacher to guide them properly and adopt remedial measures to eliminate their weak points.

Essay Type Tests in Commerce Subjects

As in other subjects so also in commerce essay type tests are quite commonly used for evaluation purposes. Such tests have certain merits and demerits.

Merits of Essay-type Tests

(i) Such tests induce good study habits in the pupils.

(ii) The guess work can be eliminated to large extent.

(iii) By this type of tests it is possible to measure all degrees of comprehensiveness and accuracy.

(iv) Such tests are easier to prepare and administer.

(v) These help in developing the power of logical thinking, critical reasoning, systematic presentation etc. in the students.

(vi) This type of tests are considered to be best for measuring ability to organise idea effectively, ability to criticise or justify a statement, ability to interpret etc.

(vii) Such tests can be used by all type of schools.

(vii) Such tests provide an opportunity to the child to show his initiative, or, fertility of their imagination, etc.

Defects of Essay-type Tests

At present new type of tests are taking the place of traditional or Essay type of tests. This trend is gaining importance because traditional type of examinations suffer from following defects.

(a) Defects from the Point of View of Students

(i) The essay type tests are less objective and so they lack of validity. This type of test can reveal child's cramming capacity only.

(ii) These tests lack reliability. A students is compelled to have a selective reading. He depends more on guess papers and so there is an element of chance.

(iii) It keeps the students busy and full of nervous tension. The study does not spread over the whole year and is limited to a short period just before the examinations. Thus a habit of irregular study is developed in the student.

(b) Defects of Essay-type Tests from the Point of View of the Teacher

(i) The teacher covers only a limited and important portion of course because his aim is to see that maximum number of his students pass the examination.

(ii) The teaching programme of the teacher is wholly examination oriented and the basic principle of teaching his students are given least consideration.

(iii) Since a teacher is judged by the results of his students so every thing becomes subservient to the examinations.

(iv) To show good results some times the teacher devotes a good deal of his time to indulge in guess work which affects his teaching.

(v) The teacher is compelled to encourage his students to cramming which is not a psychological method of teaching.

***(c)* Defects from the Point of View of Achievement**

(i) Essay type tests are not comprehensive and some students may get good marks only because the questions have been set from the portion prepared by them.

(ii) This type of tests are not useful from the point of view of improvement. They fail to throw light on the defects of teaching-learning process or the defects of the curriculum.

(iii) These tests are not objective and the score of a student depends on various factors such as Examiners mood and whims etc.

From the above it can be concluded that essay type examination is not a correct method of evaluation in commerce. The improvement in system of evaluation is possible if following suggestions are given due consideration.

***(a)* Improvement in Essay Type Examination.** In essay type examination an improvement is possible if we set shorter questions spread over the whole course. The language of question should be clear and precise clear cut directions be given for scoring.

***(b)* The Use of Objective Tests.** In addition to essay type tests, some objective type tests may also be used for evaluation. The objective type tests can be of the following types:

(i) True-false type.

(ii) Completion type.

(iii) Multiple choice type.

(iv) Matching type.

(v) Short answer type.

***(c)* Use of Oral Tests.** In such tests oral questions are given and students are required to give answers after oral calculations. Such tests require quick recall and thinking the ability of the students to apply the knowledge of facts in different situations.

***(d)* Assessment of Regular Work.** For such an assessment a record of child's developments should be kept. Such a record may be kept for his home-work, practical work etc. and this should be taken into consideration while assessing a student.

Thus we find that no single device is enough and a judicious blend of various evaluation tools is the best approach.

Objective Tests in Commerce

At present objective tests are used for evaluation. The objective tests consist of completion type tests, matching type tests, True/False type tests etc. Such objective tests have following merits:

(i) The objective tests have little or no scope of subjectivity. The score does not depend of Examiner's mood or whims.

(ii) These are comprehensive. This requires from the students, thorough study of the syllabus.

(iii) These tests are more reliable. The score does not depend on expression, speed, style etc.

(iv) These are easy to administer and easy to score.

(v) There is no chance element in this type of tests.

(vi) These are economical in respect of time.

However, they also suffer from certain drawbacks. Some of these are as under:

(i) The objective type tests fails to test the organising ability of the students.

(ii) These tests fail to develop thinking and reasoning powers of the students which is one of the main aims of teaching commerce.

(iii) These tests put more emphasis on factual knowledge and very little knowledge and importance is given to processes, methods or originality of thought.

(iv) These tests encourage guess work.

(v) These tests are not diagnostic. Because they do not show the defects in the teaching-learning process.

(vi) It needs a lot of time and labour for preparing such a test.

(vii) These tests may pose some administrative difficulties as there may be indiscipline in the students. They may use unfair means, wishper answers or make some gestures.

Different Types of Objective Test. We have already seen the various types of objective tests. Let-us now describe each of them in some detail.

1. Completion Type of Test or Memory Recall. This type of test consists of questions that are either sentences or statements, in between the words a blank is left within the body of the material. Sometimes the space is left in the margin which has to filled in by the students.

In this type of tests words used are quite important and so the statement or the question should be worded carefully leaving no scope for ambiguity. If the students get confused the very purpose of such a test is lost.

2. True and False Type. In this type, a number of statements are given. Some of these are true and some are false. The students are required to tick or write 'yes' before a correct statement. Such a test is not difficult to construct but while constructing such a test the care be taken not to put very deceptive statements before the students.

3. Multiple Choice Tests. The multiple choice test contains a number of items, each of which has two or three responses. One of the responses in each item is correct. Two students are required to tick the correct response. This type of test requires memory as also the correct knowledge and a good vocabulary.

4. Matching Type Tests. In these tests, in each item, there are two columns relevant. Each items in the first column is to be matched with the relevant item of the second column, not given in the same order. To avoid guess work, the items in the second column or more or less in it than the items in the first column.

5. Classification Type of Test. In this type of test such questions are set which contain certain groups of work. Every group contains about five words out of which one is the correct answer to the question. The correct word has to be underlined. In fact, it involves memory recognition as well as recall.

A thoughful consideration of essay type and objective type test reveals that we should use both type of test for evaluation. Depending upon what teacher wants to assess he should decide which type of test will be more useful in assessing the same. For removal of any guess work in objective type tests, the following formula is useful:

$$\text{Score} = R - W/N - 1$$

where, R = number of right responses.

W = number of wrong responses

N = number of alternative responses.

Requirements of the Type of Test. New type of tests have to be carefully constructed. The following precautions be taken otherwise, these tests are likely to lose the utility:

(1) Careful planning and construction.

(2) These test should be carefully planned and constructed only then they shall serve their purpose. For this the following things are needed:

(a) ***Determination of the Purpose.*** The basic purpose of the test must be decided first.

(b) ***Selection of the Test in Accordance with the Purpose.*** After the purpose has been decided, the test has to be found out which would suit the purpose.

(c) ***Objective Questions.*** The question that are constructed should be objective.

(d) ***Scoring Key to be Prepared.*** The scoring key, that provides answers to the questions, must also be prepared. Unless it is done, the purpose shall not be served. Without this, it shall be difficult to award marks.

(e) ***Standardisation.*** These tests need standardisation. Then only is possible to do away with the element of subjectivity.

(f) ***Ability of the Students to be Kept in Mind.*** The individual differences and the mental ability of the students should be kept in mind. Otherwise the purpose shall not be served.

(g) ***Intelligent Planning.*** It is not possible for all teachers to plan these tests. These tests have to be planned and constructed by intelligent teachers as they require intelligent planning.

Other Types of Tests. In addition to the tests given above, the following types of tests are also used.

(a) ***Intelligence Test.*** The basic object of these tests is to ascertain the mental capacity or the psychological capacity of the students. These tests require such questions that would give an idea about the mental age of the students.

(b) ***Recognition Test.*** These tests have element of the traditional examination as also the new system of examination. In these tests, a figure is drawn or a particular question is given and the students have to recognise it.

(c) ***Logical Selection Test.*** In this test, several names of a particular object are given. The correct and the exact name is to be sorted out by the students. This is also a new type of test.

10

Methods of Teaching Accountancy

Accountancy is a business language. It speaks about the business affairs. To make the business language convey same meaning every where, it has been developed around some commonly accepted ideas. These ideas are called accounting concepts. The important accounting concepts are:

(1) Business Entity Concept. This concept suggests that business is an entity in itself. It is separate from its owner. The owner should not mix up his family or private affairs with the business affairs. He should keep his personal or household expense and income separate from the business expense or income. The owner should record his transactions with his own business, as he records the transactions with the outsiders. Business entity concept helps to judge business performance separately.

(2) Money Measurement Concept. This concept suggets that in Accountancy transactions or events are measured and recorded in money. That is in rupee or any other monetary unit. The events which are not measurable in money are not recorded.

(3) Cost Concept. This concept suggests that in accountancy all transactions should be recorded at actual cost. They should not be recorded at imaginery cost, unless it is unavoidable. This concept prevents assets and transactions being over valued or undervalued. In short the cost concept helps us to record actual facts based on cost. It makes accounting more reliable and accurate.

(4) Going Concern Concept. This concept suggests that accounts should be prepared as a long time record. We should presume that the business will continue indefinitely or it is a going concern. The concept of going concern makes us to provide for depreciation on various assets and create reserves for expected losses systematically. It also makes us to treat good will and prepaid expenses as assets.

(5) Duel Aspect Concept. This concept suggests that every business transaction has duel aspect or two sides: *(a)* Receiving of benefit and *(b)* Giving of benefit. When we purchase a machine we make a transnction. In this transaction we receive the machine benefit and give the money benefit, as its price. These two benefits when measured in terms of money are equal. That is:

Benefit received = Benefit given

Thus in every transaction one benefit is received and in exchange some other benefit is given. In other words, each transaction creates a receiver and a giver of benefit. The receiver becomes a debtor and the giver the creditor. For one, who receives something, will have to return something in exchange to the person from whom he has received the thing. So, to make a complete record of each transaction it is recorded in two accounts. The debtor's account and the creditors account. This is why the system of writing accounts is called Double entry system.

When ever we purchase an asset, we pay it out of our capital or accept a liability to pay. Therefore:

Assets = Capital + Liabilities

or

Capital = Assets – Liabilities

The whole structure of Accountancy is based on duel aspect concept of business transaction.

(6) Matching Concept. This concept suggests that profit or loss is the difference between income earned and the expenses incurred during a certain period. Thus calculation of profit or loss is. based on the maching concept of revenue earned and the expenses incurred. That is:

Profit = Income earned – Expenses incurred

Loss = Expenses incurred – Income earned

(7) Realisation Concept. This concept suggests that Accountancy should record only, what is realised or achieved. It should not anticipate future events such as sales or income and exagerate the firms profit. Profit should be taken for granted only when it is realised in cash or some party has accepted the liability to pay. But as a precaution anticipated losses such as bad debts are taken into account and for which reserves are created.

(8) Accrual Concept. This concept suggests that transaction which yet not settled in cash should also be taken into account to ascertain profit or loss. In other words accrued income, as well as accrued expenses should also form a basis for calculation of profit or loss. Accrued income is an income which is not received in cash but a claim is established. In the same way accrued expense is an expense which is not paid but a liability is established.

Accounting Conventions

Convention means custom or tradition. Accounting conventions are related to Accounting records. These conventions provide useful guidance in preparing accounts or financial statements. The important conventions are:

(1) Convention of Consistency. According to this convention, the accounting records should be consistent. In other words, they should remain similar in form and contents unless a change is unavoidable. Consistency of records help in making comparison between past and present business results. If the form and contents of records are often changed, the comparison becomes difficult and the value of accounting records decrease.

(2) Convention of Full Disclosure. According to this convention, the accounts should reveal all important financial information, necessary for the business. It should fulfil the aims of accounting, and help in business management.

(3) Convention of Conservatism. According to this convention we should be conservative or careful in calculating profit. Profit should never be anticipated and exagerated. But losses should be anticipated and provided. For Profit should be calculated net of all the possible losses. It must be certain and minimum.

(4) Convention of Materiality. Materiality means importance. Materiality of a transaction depends on the amount of money it involves. According to materiality convention small payments should be treated as expenses but big payments of permanent nature should be treated as assets. The financial statements should be presented only in round figures, say in rupees, and paise being immaterial should be left out.

Accounting Systems

Accounting system refer to Accounting methods. There are different Accounting systems. These are:

(1) Cash System. Under this system only cash transactions are recorded. Credit transactions are not recorded, until cash is actually paid or received. This system does not recognise accrual concept. Cash system of accountancy is generally adopted by non-trading concerns such as temples, clubs, or schools. It is also adopted by professional men like doctors and lawyers.

(2) Mercantile System. This system is generally adopted by merchants. Under this system cash as well as credit transactions are recorded. This system recognises the accrual concept of Accounting. It records amounts paid and received as well as the amounts to be paid and to be received.

(3) Single Entry System. This system does not recognise the duel aspect concept of accounting. In this system two sides of each transaction are not recorded. It generally records, only the personal side of each trasaction. This system is inaccurate, incomplete and unscientific. This system is adopted by small shop keepers, either because of their ignorance or because they think that, accurate business information is not necessary or worth while.

(4) Double Entry System. This system recognises the duel aspect concept of each transaction. It records each transanction in two accounts representing two aspects of the transaction. This system is the most scientific perfect, and accurate. It provides all the necessary business information. It is the only universal system of Accountancy widely adopted and practiced. This book is ment for the study of Double entry Accountancy.

(5) Indian System. This system of Accountancy called "*Deshi Nama*", is a bit changed form of Double entry system. This system is also perfect and scientific. It is older and easier than the Double entry system. *Deshi Nama* is practiced through out India in different Indian languages.

Importance of Accounting

Accounting provides very useful information to the following parties:

(1) The Owner. The person who owns business, wants to know whether his money is properly used. For this he must see the financial statements of the business. Accounting provides all such statements.

(2) The Investor. The investor who invests money in a running business should be assured that his money will be properly utilised. For this the investors need to study the accounting records of the firm. The Accounting records revel the true nature of the business.

(3) The Creditor. The Creditor is a person, who supply goods and services to the business on credit. He also advances loans. So before he enters into such contracts he should ascertain the earning capacity of the business and its ability to meet its obligation. Accounting provides the necessary information to the creditor.

(4) The Manager. Accounting records reveal financial operation of the business. So these records are useful in the direction and control of business. Based on the accounting records the manager fixes responsibilities and judge the performance of the staff. Providing guidance in management in one of the principal functions of Accountancy.

(5) The Research Scholar. Accounting records specially the financial statements are useful to the research scholar. They help in the study of financial operation of the firm.

(6) The Government. The Government levies tax on the profit of the business. So the Government needs financial statements of such business to ascertain the profit. The Government also needs accounting statistics, to formulate its policy towards trade and industry.

Principles of Debiting and Crediting

The trader keeps with him accounts of all those persons with whom he deals. These persons include individuals and institutions. These accounts are called personal accounts. They show how much the trader owes to various persons or they owe to him.

Each account is vertically divided into two halves. The left half is called the debit side and is denoted by 'Dr.' The right half is called the credit side and is denoted by 'Cr.' Amounts of transactions by which a person becomes a debtor are written in the debit side of his account. This is called 'debiting an account'. Similarly amounts of transactions by which a person becomes creditor are written in the credit side of his account. This is called 'crediting an account'.

The trader has separate accounts for each of his customers. If at any time the total of the debit side in an account is greater than the total in the credit side then the person concerned is a debtor to the trader. On the other hand if the total of the credit side in an account is greater than the total in the debt side then the person concerned is a creditor to the trader.

When a person receives something he becomes debtor of the person, who gives him the thing. On the other hand when a person gives something he becomes creditor of the person, whom the thing is given. So, in any transaction the account of a person is debited when he receives something and credited when he gives something. In other words personal accounts are debited when they receive something and credited when they give something.

Just as personal accounts the trader keeps separate account for each of his assets; such as building, machinery or furniture. Accounts of assets are called real accounts or property accounts. They show the present value of the concerned asset. The real account has also a debit side and a credit side. Whenever an asset is purchased its value is debited and whenever it is sold its value is credited into its account. Debit side total in a real account shows the total amount spent and the total of the credit side shows the total amount realised from the asset. At any time if we substract the credit side amount from the debit side amount we get the present value of the concerned asset. Real accounts are debited when things are purchased or brought in and credited when they are sold out or given away.

The trader also keeps the accounts of different sources of income and expenditure such as rent, interest and wages. These are called nominal accounts or accounts of income and expenses. Nominal account has also a debit side and a credit side. When an amount is spent it is debited in the concerned nominal account. On the other hand when an income is received it is credited in the concerned nominal accoount. The debit side total of a nominal account shows the total expenses incurred on it and the credit side total shows the total amount received from it.

The principles of debiting and crediting different types of account can be stated as:

1. In personal account debit the receiver and credit the giver.
2. In real account debit what comes in & credit what goes out.
3. In nominal account debit expenses and credit gains.

Important Points to be Noted in Writing Accounts

1. Every transaction has two sides a debit side and a credit side. So when a transaction is completed it is recorded in two different accounts. One account is debited and the other account is credited.

2. Each transaction should be considered independently and then it should be recorded. Suppose we purchase goods worth Rs. 100 from Ram on credit and then on due date we

make its payment. In this case the purchase of goods should be considered as one transaction and its payment should be considered as another transaction. So when purchases are made it should be recorded into two accounts and when its payment is made it should also be recorded into two accounts. In other words purchases from Ram and its subsequent payment should be treated as two separated transactions.

3. Various transactions of the trader made him a debtor or a creditor. As such the trader can open his one account and enter all his transactions into it. But the trader needs detailed information abount his transactions. So he enters different transactions related to him in different accounts. He opens for himself separate accounts, relating to purchases, sales, wages, salary, interest, building, furniture etc. In other words the trader does not write all his transactions in one account but in a number of accounts.

The book in which various accounts are kept is called 'Ledger'. A number is given to each account and one index is prepared for reference. The ledger is the Principal Book of account. It contains all personal, real and nominal accounts. The proforma of an Account is:

Dr. **Name and Account Number** **Cr.**

Date	*Particulars*	*L.F.*	*Amount*		*Date*	*Particulars*	*L.F.*	*Amount*	
			Rs.	*Ps.*				*Rs.*	*Ps.*

Thus it can be seen that the name and the number of the account is written on the top of the account. If an account becomes debtor by a transaction then it is entered in the debit side and if it becomes a creditor it is entered in the credit side of the account. The date of the transaction is entered in the date column, particulars in the particular column; ledger folio of the other connected account in the Ledger folio column, and the amount in the amount column.

The Journal and Transations

All business transactions are first entered in a book, called 'Journal' and then they are transfered to various ledger accounts, Journal is a book in which transactions are entered one after another as and when they are made. All transactions made on a particular date are found under that date. Writing of transactions in journal is called 'Journalising'. From journal transactions are sorted out and entered in the concerned ledger accounts. This is called, 'Ledger posting' .

A transaction has two sides, the debit side and the credit side. In journal both sides are recorded.

The journal is ruled like this:

Date	*Particulars*	*L.F.*	*Debit Amount Rs.*	*Credit Amount Rs.*

The date of the transaction is entered in the date column. In the particulars column first we write the name of the debtor account and just below it, the name of the creditor account. In the L.F. (Ledger folio) column we enter the folio or the page numbers of the two accounts. The amount of the transaction is entered in the debit and credit columns in front of the concerned accounts.

Leadger Posting

Transactions are entered in the journal in the order in which they take place. Transactions of a similar nature (*i.e.* transactions relating to a particular account) may be entered in the different pages of the journal if they take place on different dates. One cannot know the net effect of similar transactions (*i.e.* the actual position of an account) on any particular date with the help of the journal. It is, therefore, necessary to classify the various transactions entered in the journal and bring transactions of a similar nature in one place. For instance, all the transactions relating to cash must be brought together in one place. Similarly, all the transactions relating to a particular customer must be grouped together in one place. The grouping of transactions of a similar nature is done by a process known as "posting". Posting is the act of transferring the transactions from the journal to the second book called the ledger. Since all the transactions relating to a particular account (*i.e.* transactions of a similar nature) appear in a summarised and classified form in the ledger, one can find out the exact position of each account on any date.

Features of Ledger

The ledger is the principal book of accounts because it is from this book that a trader can obtain final information relating to the financial position of his business. It is also known as the book of final entry because all business transactions are entered first in the journal and finally in the ledger.

The ledger is a book which contains accounts. An account is a summarised record of business transactions relating to a particular person, property or service. The ledger has an account for every person with whom the concern deals, for every asset held by the concern and for every item of expense incurred or income earned by the concern. Thus there are three types of accounts in the ledger, *viz.*, (1) personal accounts, (2) real accounts and (3) nominal accounts.

In the ledger, each account is allotted one or more pages depending upon the number of transactions relating to that account.

Each ledger account is divided into two sides, *viz.* (1) left hand side and (2) right hand side. The left hand side is called the "debit side" and the right hand side is called the "credit side".

The debit aspect of a transaction will be entered on the debit side of the account and the credit aspect of a transaction will be entered on the credit side of the account. In other words, if an account receives any benefit, it will be entered on the debit side of that account and if it gives any benefit, it will be entered on the credit side of that account.

Ruling of Ledger

A ledger account is ruled as follows:

Account

Dr. Cr.

Date 1	*Particulars* 2	*Folio* 3	*Amount* 4	*Date* 1	*Particulars* 2	*Folio* 3	*Amount* 4
			Rs.				*Rs.*

The first column (Date) is meant for entering the date of the transaction.

The second column (particulars) is meant for entering the details of the transaction.

The third column (Folio) is meant for entering the page number of the journal from which the transaction is transferred.

The fourth column (Amount) is meant for entering the amount.

Points to be Noted While Preparing the Ledger Accounts

The following points should be noted while preparing the ledger accounts:

1. In the ledger, a separate account should be opened for every account that is found in the journal.
2. A new account of the same name must not be opened for every transaction. All the transactions relating to a particular account should be entered in the account already opened.
3. The name of the account should be written in bold letters at the top and in the centre of each account.
4. The word "Dr". (abbreviation of debit) should be written at the left hand top corner of each account. The word "Cr". (abbreviation of credit) should be written at the right hand top corner of each account.
5. Each account should have sufficient space for posting all the entries relating to that account.
6. The journal entries should be posted to the ledger accounts in the order of their dates.
7. While posting, the name of the account in which an entry is posted should not appear in that very account.
8. The date of each item should be entered in the date column against the entry.

9. On the debit side, every entry in the particulars column must begin with the word "To". On the credit side, every entry in the particulars column must begin with the word "By".

10. The account which is debited in the journal should be posted on the debit side of the concerned ledger account. The account which is credited in the journal should be posted on the credit side of the concerned ledger account.

11. While posting on the debit side of an account, the name of the account which is credited in the journal should be written in the particulars column. Similarly, while posting on the credit side of an account, the name of the account which is debited in the journal should be written in the 'Particulars column.'

12. The page number of the journal from where an entry is posted should be written in the 'Folio' column.

13. The nature of the currency (such as Rs. Ps. or £.s.d.) in which the account is kept, should be written in the amount columns.

14. Every ledger account must be balanced at the end of every month or any other fixed period.

Balancing of Ledger Accounts

We have studied earlier that every ledger account has two sides, *viz.* (1) the debit side and (2) the credit side. The benefits received by an account are entered on its debit side and the benefits given by an account are entered on its credit side. Now the question arises as to whether a particular account has received more benefits than it has given or *vice versa* on any particular date. In order to find out whether a particular account has received more benefits than It has given or *vice versa,* it is necessary to balance that account on a given date. The process of ascertaining the balance of a particular account on a given date is known as "Balancing the account" or "Striking the balance".

In order to balance an account, one should total up the two sides of the concerned account roughly on a separate sheet of paper and find out the difference between the two totals. The difference between the two totals is then entered in the amount column of the lighter side to make both the sides equal. While entering the difference in the amount column of the lighter side, the words "To Balance carried down" or "By Balance carried down" should be written against the amount in the 'particulars' column. After inserting the balance on the lighter side, the two sides are totalled and lines are drawn above and below the totals. Then the balance is written on the opposite side with the words "To Balance brought down" or "By Balance brought down" in the 'particulars' column. This balance represents the starting point of the account for the next period.

In the context of balancing of ledger accounts, it should be noted that when nominal accounts are balanced on the last date of a financial year, their balances are not carried down but are transferred to Profit and Loss Account.

A ledger account may show a debit balance or a credit balance. If the debit side total of a ledger account is greater than its credit side total, the difference is called a debit balance. If the credit side total of a ledger account is greater than its debit side total, the difference is called a credit balance.

A debit balance on a personal account indicates that the person concerned has received more benefits from the business concern than what he has given to the business concern. Therefore, the person concerned owes the amount of the balance to the business concern. A credit balance on a personal account indicates that the person concerned has given more benefits to the business concern than what he has received from the business concern. Therefore, the business concern owes the amount of the balance to the person concerned.

A debit balance on a real account represents the value of the particular property. A real account other than sales account and purchases returns account will not show a credit balance except when the asset concerned is sold at a profit.

A debit balance on a nominal account indicates the amount of expense or loss under that item. A credit balance on a nominal account indicates the amount of income or gain under that item.

The proprietor's capital account will show a credit balance and his drawings account will show a debit balance.

The manner in which the various transactions, after being entered in the journal, are posted to the ledger is explained in the following illustration:

Illustration 1.

Journalise the following transactions and post them in the various ledger accounts.

	2002			Rs.
1.	Jan.	1	Rao commenced business with	5,000
2.	Jan.	2	Bought goods for cash	2,500
3.	Jan.	3	Bought office furniture for cash	500
4.	Jan.	4	Paid for postage	10
5.	Jan.	5	Purchased goods from Rajkumar	2,000
6.	Jan.	7	Sold goods for cash	150
7.	Jan.	8	Bought goods from Rahim	400
8.	Jan.	9	Sold goods to Suresh	400

9.	Jan. 10	Sold goods to Nayak	300
10.	Jan. 11	Purchased goods for cash	350
11.	Jan. 13	Received cash from Nayak	250
12.	Jan. 15	Paid cash to Rahim	400
13.	Jan. 17	Returned goods to Rajkumar	200
14.	Jan. 20	Suresh returned goods	50
15.	Jan. 22	Paid Salaries	150
16.	Jan. 25	Sold goods for cash	500
17.	Jan. 26	Rao withdrew for personal use	800
18.	Jan. 27	Paid for stationery	100
19.	Jan. 28	Paid rent	225
20.	Jan. 31	Received commission	50

Solution.

The journal entries for the above transactions are as follows:

	Date	*Particulars*	*L.F.*	*Debit Amount Rs.*	*Credit Amount Rs.*
(1)	*(2)*	*(3)*	*(4)*	*(5)*	*(6)*
	2002				
1.	Jan. 1	Cash A/c Dr.		5,000	
		To Capital A/c			5,000
		(Being the Capital brought in by Rao)			
2.	Jan. 2	Purchases A/c Dr.		2,500	
		To Cash A/c			2,500
		(Being the goods bought for cash)			

(1)	(2)	(3)	(4)	(5)	(6)
3.	Jan. 3	Office Furniture A/c Dr.		500	
		To Cash A/c			500
		(Being the office furniture bought for cash)			
4.	Jan. 4	Postage A/c Dr.		10	
		To Cash A/c			10
		(Being the cash paid for postage)			
5.	Jan. 5	Purchase A/c Dr.		2,000	
		To Rajkumar's A/c			2,000
		(Being the goods bought from Rajkumar on credit)			
6.	Jan. 7	Cash A/c Dr.		150	
		To Sales A/c			150
		(Being the goods sold by cash)			
7.	Jan. 8	Purchases A/c Dr.		400	
		To Rahim's A/c			400
		(Being the goods bought from Rahim on credit)			
8.	Jan. 9	Suresh's A/c Dr.		400	
		To Sales A/c			400
		(Being the goods sold to Suresh on credit)			
9.	Jan. 10	Nayak's A/c Dr.		300	
		To Sales A/c			300
		(Being the goods sold to Nayak on credit)			
10.	Jan. 11	Purchases A/c Dr.		350	
		To Cash A/c			350
		(Being the goods purchased for cash)			

(1)	*(2)*	*(3)*		*(4)*	*(5)*	*(6)*
11.	Jan. 13	Cash A/c	Dr.		250	
		To Nayak's A/c				250
		(Being the cash received from Nayak on credit)				
12.	Jan. 15	Rahim's A/c	Dr.		400	
		To Cash A/c				400
		(Being the cash paid to Rahim)				
13.	Jan. 17	Rajkumar's A/c	Dr.		200	
		To Purchases Returns A/c				200
		(Being the goods returned to Rajkumar)				
14.	Jan. 20	Sales Returns A/c	Dr.		50	
		To Suresh's A/c				50
		(Being the goods returned by Suresh)				
15.	Jan. 22	Salaries A/c	Dr.		150	
		To Cash A/c				150
		(Being the cash paid for salaries)				
16.	Jan. 25	Cash A/c	Dr.		500	
		To Sales A/c				500
		(Being the goods sold for cash)				
17.	Jan. 26	Drawings A/c	Dr.		800	
		To Cash A/c				800
		(Being the cash withdrawn by Rao for his personal use)				
18.	Jan. 27	Stationery A/c	Dr.		100	
		To Cash A/c				100
		(Being the cash paid for stationery)				

(1)	(2)	(3)		(4)	(5)	(6)
19.	Jan. 28	Rent A/c	Dr.		225	
		To Cash A/c				225
		(Being the cash paid for rent)				
20.	Jan. 31	Cash A/c	Dr.		50	
		To Commission A/c				50
		(Being the cash received for commission)				

The above journal entries are posted to the various ledger accounts in the following manner:

Dr. **Capital Account** Cr.

2002		Rs.	2002		Rs.
Jan. 31	To Balance c/d	5,000	Jan. 1	By Cash A/c	5,000
		5,000			5,000
			Feb. 1	By Balance b/d	5,000

Dr. **Drawings Account** Cr.

2002		Rs.	2002		Rs.
Jan. 26	To Cash A/c	800	Jan. 31	By Balance c/d	800
		800			800
Feb. 1	To Balance b/d	800			

Dr. **Purchases Account** Cr.

2002		Rs.	2002		Rs.
Jan. 2	To Cash A/c	2,500	Jan. 31	By Balance c/d	5,250
Jan. 5	To Rajkumar's A/c	2,000			
Jan. 8	To Rahim's A/c	400			
Jan. 11	To Cash A/c	350			
		5,250			5,250
Feb. 1	To Balance b/d	5,250			

Dr. **Sales Account** Cr.

2002		Rs.	2002		Rs.
Jan. 31	To Balance b/d	1,350	Jan. 7	By Cash A/c	350
			Jan. 9	By Suresh's A/c	400
			Jan. 10	By Nayak's A/c	300
			Jan. 25	By Cash A/c	500
		1,350			1,350
			Feb. 1	By Balance b/d	1,350

Dr. **Purchases Returns Account** Cr.

2002		Rs.	2002		Rs.
Jan. 31	To Balance c/d	200	Jan. 17	By Rajkumar's A/c	200
		200			200
			Feb. 1	By Balance b/d	200

Dr. **Sales Returns Account** Cr.

2002		Rs.	2002		Rs.
Jan. 20	To Suresh's A/c	50	Jan. 31	By Balance c/d	50
		50			50
Feb. 1	To Balance b/d	200			

Dr. **Office Furniture Account** Cr.

2002		Rs.	2002		Rs.
Jan. 3	To Cash A/c	500	Jan. 31	By Balance c/d	500
		500			500
Feb. 1	To Balance b/d	50			

Dr. **Cash Account** Cr.

2002		Rs.	2002		Rs.
Jan. 1	To Capital A/c	5,000	Jan. 2	By Purchases A/c	2,500
Jan. 7	To Sales A/c	150	Jan. 3	By Office Furniture A/c	500
Jan. 13	To Nayak's A/c	250	Jan. 4	By Postage A/c	10
Jan. 25	To Sales A/c	500	Jan. 11	By Purchases A/c	350
Jan. 31	To Commission A/c	50	Jan. 15	By Rahim's A/c	400
			Jan. 22	By Salaries A/c	150
			Jan. 26	By Drawings A/c	800
			Jan. 27	By Stationery A/c	100
			Jan. 28	By Rent A/c	225
			Jan. 31	By Balance c/d	915
		5,950			5,950
Feb. 1	To Balance b/d	915			

Dr. **Rajkumar's Account** Cr.

2002		Rs.	2002		Rs.
Jan. 17	To Purchases Returns A/c	200	Jan. 5	By Purchases A/c	2,000
Jan. 31	To Balance c/d	1,800			
		2,000			2,000
			Feb. 1	By Balance b/d	1,800

Dr. **Rahim's Account** Cr.

2002		Rs.	2002		Rs.
Jan. 15	To Cash A/c	400	Jan. 8	By Purchases A/c	400
		400			400

Dr. **Suresh's Account** Cr.

2002		Rs.	2002		Rs.
Jan. 9	To Sales A/c	400	Jan. 20	By Sales Returns A/c	50
			Jan. 31	By Balance c/d	350
		400			400
Feb. 1	To Balance b/d	350			

Dr. **Nayak's Account** Cr.

2002		Rs.	2002		Rs.
Jan. 10	To Sales A/c	300	Jan. 13	By Sales Returns A/c	250
			Jan. 31	By Balance c/d	50
		300			300
Feb. 1	To Balance b/d	50			

Dr. **Postage Account** Cr.

2002		Rs.	2002		Rs.
Jan. 4	To Cash A/c	10	Jan. 31	By Balance c/d	10
		10			10
Feb. 1	To Balance b/d	10			

Dr. **Salaries Account** Cr.

2002		Rs.	2002		Rs.
Jan. 22	To Cash A/c	150	Jan. 31	By Balance c/d	150
		150			150
Feb. 1	To Balance b/d	150			

Dr. **Stationery Account** Cr.

2002		Rs.	2002		Rs.
Jan. 27	To Cash A/c	100	Jan. 31	By Balance c/d	100
		100			100
Feb. 1	To Balance b/d	100			

Dr. **Rent Account** Cr.

2002		Rs.	2002		Rs.
Jan. 28	To Cash A/c	225	Jan. 31	By Balance A/c	225
		225			225
Feb. 1	To Balance b/d	225			

Dr. **Commission Account** Cr.

2002		Rs.	2002		Rs.
Jan. 31	To Balance c/d	50	Jan. 31	By Cash A/c	50
		50			50
			Feb. 1	By Balance b/d	50

Explanation of Posting

1. In this entry, cash account and capital account are affected. So posting should be made in these two accounts. Since cash account is to be debited, we should write (in the particulars column) on the debit side of cash account "To capital account". Since capital account is to be credited, we should write (in the particulars column) on the credit side of capital account "By cash account".

2. In this entry, purchases account and cash account are affected. So posting should be made in these two accounts. Since purchases account is to be debited, we should write (in

the particulars column) on the debit side of purchases account "To cash account". Since cash account is to be credited, we should write (in the particulars column) on the credit side of cash account "By purchases account".

3. In this entry, office furniture account and cash account are involved. So posting must be made in these two accounts. Since office furniture account is to be debited, we should write (in the particulars column) on the debit side of office furniture account "To cash account." Since cash account is to be credited, we should write (in the particulars column) on the credit side of cash account "By office furniture account".

4. In this entry, postage account and cash account are affected. So posting must be made in these two accounts. Since postage account is to be debited, we should write (in the particulars column) on the debit side of postage account "To cash account". Since cash account is to be credited, we must write (in the particulars column) on the credit side of cash account "By postage account".

5. In this entry, purchases account and Rajkumar's account are affected. So posting should be made in these two accounts. Since purchases account is to be debited, we should write (in the particulars column) on the debit side of purchases account "To Rajkumar's account". Since Rajkumar's account is to be credited, we should write (in the particulars column) on the credit side of Rajkumar's account "By purchases account".

6. In this entry, cash account and sales account are affected. So posting must be made in these two accounts. Since cash account is to be debited, we must write (in the particulars column) on the debit side of cash account. "To sales account". Since sales account is to be credited, we should write (in the particulars column) on the credit side of sales account. "By cash account".

7. In this entry, purchases account and Rahim's account are affected. So posting must be made in these two accounts. Since purchases account is to be debited, we should write (in the particulars column) on the debit side of purchases account "To Rahim's account". Since Rahim's account is to be credited, we should write (in the particulars column) on the credit side of Rahlm's account "By purchases account".

8. In this entry, Suresh's account and sales account are affected. So posting must be made in these two accounts. Since Suresh's account is to be debited, we must write (in the particulars column) on the debit side of Suresh's account "To sales account". Since sales account is to be credited, we should write (in the particulars column) on the credit side of sales account "By Suresh's account".

9. In this entry, Nayak's account and sales account are affected. So posting should be made in these two accounts. Since Nayak's account is to be debited, we must write (in the particulars column) on the debit side of Nayak's account "To sales account". Since sales account is to be credited, we must write (in the particulars column) on the credit side of sales account "By Nayak's account."

10. In this entry, purchases account and cash account are affected. So posting must be made in these two accounts. Since purchases account is to be debited, we should write (in the particulars column) on the debit side of purchases account "To cash account". Since cash account is to be credited, we should write (in the particulars column) on the credit side of cash account "By purchases account".

11. In this entry, cash account and Nayak's account are affected. So posting must be made in these two accounts. Since cash account is to be debited, we should write (in the particulars column) on the debit side of cash account "To Nayak's account." Since Nayak's account is to be credited, we must write (in the particulars column) on the credit side of Nayak's account "By cash account".

12. In this entry, Rahim's account and cash account are affected. So posting should be made in these two accounts. Since Rahim's account is to be debited, we must write (in the particulars column) on the debit side of Rahim's account "To cash account." Since cash account is to be credited, we must write (in the particulars column) on the credit side of cash account "By Rahim's account."

13. In this entry, Rajkumar's account and purchases returns account are involved. So posting should be made in these two accounts. Since Rajkumar's account is to be debited, we must write (in the particulars column) on the debit side of Rajkumar's account "To purchases returns account." Since purchases returns account is to be credited, we must write (in the particulars column) on the credit side of purchases returns account "By Rajkumar's account".

14. In this entry, sales returns account and Suresh's account are affected. So posting should be made in these two accounts. Since sales returns account is to be debited, we must write (in the particulars column) on the debit side of sales returns account "To Suresh's account." Since Suresh's account is to be credited, we must write (in the particulars column) on the credit side of Suresh's account "By sales returns account".

15. In this entry, salaries account and cash account are affected. So posting must be made in these two accounts. Since salaries account is to be debited, we must write (in the particulars column) on the debit side of salaries account "To cash account". Since cash account is to be credited, we must write (in the particulars column) on the credit side of cash account "By salaries account."

16. In this entry, cash account and sales account are affected. So posting must be made in these two accounts. Since cash account is to be debited, we must write (in the particulars column) on the debit side of cash account "To

sales account". Since sales account is to be credited, we must write (in the particulars column) on the credit side of sales account "By cash account".

17. In this entry, drawings account and cash account are affected. So posting must be made in these two accounts. Since drawings account is to be debited, we must write (in the particulars column) on the debit side of drawings account "To cash account". Since cash account is to be credited, we must write (in the particulars column) on the credit side of cash account "By drawings account".

18. In this entry, stationery account and cash account are affected. So posting must be made in these two accounts. Since stationery account is to be debited, we must write (in the particulars column) on the debit side of stationery account "To cash account".

Since cash account is to be credited, we must write (in the particulars column) on the credit side of cash account "By stationery account".

19. In this entry, rent account and cash account are affected. So posting should be made in these two accounts. Since rent account is to be debited, we must write (in the particulars column) on the debit side of rent account "To cash account." Since cash account is to be credited, we must write (in the particulars column) on the credit side of cash account "By rent account".

20. In this entry, cash account and commission account are affected. So posting must be made in these two accounts. Since cash account is to be debited, we must write (in the particulars column) on the debit side of cash account "To commission account". Since commission account is to be credited, we must write (in the particulars column) on the credit side of commission account "By cash account."

11

Teaching of Final Accounts

Having made all the necessary adjustments, the trader has to ascertain the result (*i.e.* profit or loss) of his business for a particular trading period and also the financial position (*i.e.* assets, liabilities and capital) of his business at the end of the trading period. In order to ascertain the profit or loss of his business, he has to prepare an account called "Profit and Loss Account". The Profit and Loss Account is usually divided into two sections, *viz.*, (1) Trading Account and (2) Profit and Loss Account. These two accounts may be shown separately or they may be shown as one account called "Trading and Profit and Loss Account." However, the common practice is to show them as one account. In order to know his exact financial position, he has to prepare a statement called "Balance Sheet". The Trading Account, the Profit and Loss Account and the Balance Sheet are collectively called "Final Accounts". They are called final accounts because they are prepared finally (*i.e.* after all the accounts are closed and a trial balance is prepared) and because they show the final result of the business. The final accounts are prepared from the ledger balances appearing in the trial balance and the various adjustments made at the time of the preparation of the final accounts.

Trading Account

The trading account is an account which shows the result of trading, *i.e.*, buying and selling of goods. This account shows merely the result of buying and selling of goods, *i.e.,* gross profit or gross loss on trading without taking into account the administration and selling expenses incurred in running the business.

As the trading account shows merely the result of buying and selling of goods, it is prepared from those transactions which are directly connected with the goods. Such transactions (*i.e.* transactions directly connected with the goods) are: (1) Opening stock of goods, (2) Purchases of goods, (3) Purchases returns, (4) Direct expenses incurred on goods, (5) Sales of goods, (6) Sales returns and (7) Closing stock of goods. Thus the items usually appearing in a trading account are as follows:

On the debit side of the trading account:

1. Opening Stock, *i.e.,* Stock of goods at the beginning of the trading period.
2. Purchases of goods less purchases returns.
3. Direct expenses incurred on the goods, *i.e., (a)* expenses incurred in bringing the goods purchased to the business premises such as cartage, carriage, freight, import duty, clearing charges, dock dues, excise duty, Octroi, etc. and *(b)* expenses incurred in making the goods ready for sale such as wages, power, special packing charges and other manufacturing expenses.

On the credit side of the trading account:

(1) Sales of goods less sales returns.

(2) Closing stock, *i.e.,* stock of goods at the end ofthe trading period.

The balance of the trading account represents either the gross profit or gross loss on the trading for the period. If the credit side of the trading account exceeds the debit side, the difference is called "Gross Profit". On the other hand, if the debit side of the trading account exceeds the credit side, the difference is called "Gross Loss". The gross profit or gross loss as shown by the trading account is transferred to profit and loss account.

Direct Expenses

Direct expenses are expenses incurred in procuring (*i.e.* obtaining) goods and making the goods ready for sale. The total direct expenses (*i.e.,* direct expences paid and direct expenses outstanding) must be shown on the debit side of the trading account.

The examples of direct expenses are as follows:

Cartage, Carriage and Freight

These are transport charges incurred in the movement of goods. They may be inwards or outwards. Cartage, carriage and freight inwards refer to transport charges incurred on the goods purchased. Cartage, carriage and freight inwards should be entered on the debit side of the trading account. Cartage, carriage and freight outwards refer to transport charges incurred on the goods sold. Cartage, carriage and freight outwards should be entered on the debit side of the profit and loss account. Sometimes, it is not stated whether cartage, carriage and freight are inwards or outwards. In such a case, the common practice is to treat them as inwards and enter them on the debit side of the trading account.

In this context, it should be noted that cartage, carriage and freight paid on the fixed assets purchased should not be entered on the debit side of the trading account. They should be added to the cost of the concerned fixed assets on the assets side of the Balance Sheet.

Marine Insurance

Marine insurance paid on the goods purchased should be entered on the debit side of the trading account. On the other hand, marine insurance paid on the goods sold should be entered on the debit side of the profit and loss account. If it is not clearly stated whether the marine insurance is paid on the goods purchased or sold, it can be regarded as marine insurance paid on the purchases. Therefore, it can be entered on the debit side of the trading account.

Customs Duty, Excise Duty and Octroi Duty

If these duties are paid on the goods purchased, they should be shown on the debit side of the trading account. On the other hand, if they are paid on the goods sold, they should be shown on the debit side of the profit and loss account. When it is not stated whether they are paid on the purchases or on the sales, we can regard them as duties paid on the purchases and enter them on the debit side of the trading account.

Dock Dues and Clearing Charges

If these expenses are incurred on the purchases, they must be entered on the debit side of the trading account. On the other hand, if they are incurred on the sales, they must be entered on the debit side of the profit and loss account. When it is not clearly stated whether they are paid on the purchases or on the sales, the usual practice is to treat them as expenses incurred on the purchases. Therefore, they can be shown on the debit side of the trading account.

Wages

If wages are incurred in producing goods or in making the goods purchased ready for sale, they become direct expenses and therefore, they should be entered on the debit side of the trading account. But indirect or non-manufacturing wages should be entered on the debit side of the profit and loss account. Sometimes, it is not stated whether wages are direct or indirect. In such a case, they can be regarded as direct wages, and can be entered on the debit side of the trading account. Again, sometimes, wages and salaries are combined. In such a case, we can treat them as indirect expenses and enter them on the debit side of the profit and loss account.

In the context of wages, it must be noted that wages paid to workers engaged in the erection of a machine or in the construction of a building should not be entered on the debit side of the trading account. They should be added to the value of the concerned fixed asset on the assets side of the Balance Sheet.

Fuel, Power, Gas, Oil, Water, Heating, Lighting, etc.

Fuel, power, gas and oil used for running the machines are direct expenses. Therefore, they should appear on the debit side of the trading account.

Water used in the factory is a direct expense. Therefore, it will appear on the debit side of the trading account.

Heating and lighting may be factory expenses. Factory heating and lighting will appear on the side of the trading account, whereas office heating and lighting will appear on the debit side of the profit and loss account. Sometimes, it is not stated whether heating and lighting are for the factory or for the office. In such a case, we can treat them as office heating and lighting.

Factory Expenses

Other factory expenses such as factory rent, factory insurance, etc., are direct expenses. Therefore, they have to be entered on the debit side of the trading account.

Packing Materials and Charges

Packing materials and charges necessary to make the goods ready for sale have to be treated as direct expenses, and have to be entered on the debit side of the trading account. But packing materials and charges incurred on the finished goods for their safe despatch to the customers are indirect expenses. Therefore, they have to be entered on the debit side of the profit and loss account.

Net Sales or Sales Less Sales Returns

Sales appear as the first item on the credit side of the trading account. Sales include both cash and credit sales. The total sales are shown in the inner column. Then the sales returns or returns inwards (*i.e.* returns from the customers) are deducted from the total sales. The net sales are shown in the outer column.

In this connection, it must be noted that the term 'sales' includes only the sales of goods purchased for resale or the sales of goods manufactured by the concern. Sales of investments and fixed assets (which are not usually intended for resale) should not be included under sales.

Closing Stock

The second item on the credit side of the trading account is closing stock. The closing stock represents only the stock of finished goods at the close of the trading period in the case of a trading concern. But in the case of a manufacturing concern, it represents the stock of raw materials, partly finished goods and finished goods at the close of the trading period. The closing stock generally does not appear in the trial balance. Therefore, its value has to be calculated and brought into the books of accounts. The value of closing stock is calculated by a process known as "stock taking". A list of the unsold goods is made and those unsold goods are valued at the cost price or market price whichever is lower. Then, the closing stock is brought into account by means of a journal entry debiting closing stock account and crediting trading account. The closing stock account is debited because it is an asset and it comes in when it is brought into the books of accounts of the business. The trading account is credited because the closing stock is given by the trading account of this period to the next period.

In the context of closing stock, it should be noted that the value of stamps and stationery held at the close of the period should not be included in the closing stock, and therefore, should, not be shown on the credit side of the trading account.

Profit and Loss Account

Having prepared the trading account and ascertained the gross profit or gross loss, the trader has to prepare the profit and loss account of his business. The profit and loss account is prepared to ascertain the net profit or net loss (*i.e.* the ultimate profit or loss) of the business during a particular trading period. For the preparation of the profit and loss account, the gross profit or gross loss as shown by the trading account is transferred to (*i.e.* entered in) the profit and loss account. If there is gross profit, it is entered on the credit side of the profit and loss account. If there is gross loss, it is entered on the debit side of the profit and loss account. Then all the indirect expenses of the business (*i.e.* management and selling expenses of the business which are not entered in the trading account) such as salaries, rent, rates and taxes, printing and stationery, postage and telegrams, interest paid, discount allowed, advertisement, etc., are entered on the debit side of the profit and loss account. All the non-trading incomes (*i.e.* all incomes other than those entered in the trading account) such as interest received, commission received, rent received, discount received and so on are entered on the credit side of the profit and loss account. After all the indirect expenses and non-trading incomes are entered in the profit and loss account, the profit and loss account is balanced. The balance of the profit and loss account discloses the net profit made or net loss incurred in the business during the given trading period. If the total of the credit side of the profit and loss account exceeds the total of the debit side, the balance is called "net profit". On the other hand, if the total of the debit side of the profit and loss account exceeds the credit side, the balance is called "net loss". The net profit or net loss is transferred to the capital account of the trader. If there is net profit, it is credited to the capital account of the trader.

The following is the form of profit and loss account:

Profit and Loss Account for the Period Ending..........

Dr. Cr.

	Rs.		Rs.
To Trading Account (Gross loss transferred from trading account.)	....	By Trading Account (Gross profit transferred from trading account.)	....
To Salaries	....	By Rent received	....
To Rent, rates and taxes	....	By Commission received	....
To Office heating and lighting	....	By Interest received	....
To Insurance	....	By Discount earned	....
To Bank charges	....	By Bad debts recovered	....
To Printing and stationery	....	By Interest on drawings	....
To Legal charges	....	By Capital Account (Net loss transferred to capital account.)	....

Contd.

	Rs.		Rs.
To Postage and telegrams	....		
To General expenses	....		
To Interest paid	....		
To Discount allowed	....		
To Bad debts	....		
To Repairs	....		
To Depreciation	....		
To Conunission paid	....		
To Carriage outwards	....		
To Advertisement	....		
To Travelling expenses	....		
To Interest on capital	....		
To Capital Account	....		
(Net profit transferred to capital account.)			
Rs.	....	Rs.	....

With regard to the profit and loss account, the following points must be noted:

1. While entering the expenses in the profit and loss account, care should be taken to adjust expenses incurred but not paid (*i.e.* outstanding expenses) and expenses paid in advance (*i.e.* prepaid expenses).
2. Personal expenses of the proprietor such as life insurance premium, income-tax, etc., should not be included in the profit and loss account. They should

be treated as drawings and should be deducted from the capital on the liabilities side of the Balance Sheet.

3. While entering the incomes in the profit and loss account, care should be taken to adjust the incomes earned but not received (*i.e.* outstanding incomes) and incomes received but not earned (*i.e.* incomes received in advance).

Closing Entries

We have studied earlier that the opening stock, purchases, purchases returns, direct expenses, sales, sales returns and closing stock form the basis of the trading account, and the indirect expenses and non-trading incomes form the basis of the profit and loss account. Therefore, the above items should be transferred either to the trading account or to the profit and loss account. For transfering the above items to the trading account or to the 'profit and loss account' journal entries have to be passed. The journal entries necessary for transferring all the above items (except closing stock) to the trading account or to the profit and loss account are called closing entries. These entries are called closing entries because they serve to close these accounts. The journal entry necessary for including the closing stock in the trading account is called an adjusting entry because it serves to bring the closing stock into account. It cannot be called a closing entry because it does not serve to close the closing stock account.

Before we consider the closing entries necessary in connection with the preparation of the trading account and the profit and loss account, it is essential to know the basic principle of a closing entry. The basic principle of a closing entry is that the account to be closed should be credited if it has a debit balance, and the account to which it (*i.e.* the account to be closed) is transferred should be debited. On the other hand, if the account to be closed has a credit balance, it should be debited, and the account to which it is transferred should be credited.

The various closing entries passed in connection with the preparation of the trading account and the profit and loss account are as follows:

1. For Closing the Purchases Returns Account: As regards the closing of this account, some accountants are of the opinion that it should be closed by transfer to the purchases account, and others are of the view that it should be closed by transfer to the trading account. It is advisable to close this account by transfer to the purchases account.

The entry for transferring the purchases returns account to the purchases account is as follows:

Purchases Returns Account Dr.

To Purchases Account.

Explanation of the Above Entry. The purchases returns account has a credit balance. In order to close the purchases returns account which shows a credit balance, it should be debited. As the purchases returns account is debited, the purchases account to which the purchases returns account is transferred should be credited.

2. For Closing the Sales Returns Account: While some accountants wish to close this account by transfer to the sales account, others like to close it by transfer to the trading account. It is better to close this account by transfer to the sales account.

The entry for transferring the sales returns account to the sales account is:

Sales Account Dr.

To Sales Returns Account

Explanation of the Above Entry. The sales returns account shows a debit balance. In order to close the sales returns account which has a debit balance, it should be credited. As the sales returns account is credited, the sales account to which the sales returns account is transferred should be debited.

Note. With regard to purchases returns and sales returns, it should be noted that whatever method is adopted for closing these two accounts, the purchases returns should be deducted from the total purchases, and only the net purchases should be shown in the outer column on the debit side of the trading account. Similarly, the sales returns should be deducted from the total sales, and only the net sales should be shown in the outer column on the credit side of the trading account.

3. For Closing the Accounts of Opening Stock, Purchases and Various Direct Expenses: The accounts of opening stock, purchases and various direct expenses should be closed by transfer to the trading account. For closing all these accounts, only one journal entry is passed. The closing entry passed for closing all these accounts is:

Trading Account Dr.

To Opening Stock Account

To Purchases Account (Net amount of purchases)

To Individual Direct Expense Account.

Explanation of the Above Entry. The accounts of opening stock, purchases and direct expenses have debit balances. In order to close these accounts which show debit balances, they should be credited. As these accounts are credited, the trading account to which these accounts are transferred should be debited.

4. For Closing Sales Account: The sales account has to be closed by transfer to the trading account. The entry passed for the transfer of the sales account to the trading account is:

Sales Account (Net amount of sales) Dr.

To Trading Account

Explanation of the Above Entry. The sales account has a credit balance. In order to close the sales account which has a credit balance, it should be debited. As the sales account is debited, the trading account to which the sales account is transferred should be credited.

5. For Closing the Trading Account: The trading account should be closed by transferring its ultimate balance, *i.e.* gross profit or gross loss to the profit and loss account. The entry passed for closing the trading account is:

(a) If the trading account shows a credit balance, *i.e.*, gross profit:

Trading Account Dr.

To Profit and Loss Account.

Explanation of the Entry. The trading account shows gross profit or credit balance. In order to close the trading account which shows a credit balance, it should be debited. As the trading account is debited, the profit and loss account to which the balance of the trading account is transferred should be credited.

(b) If the trading account shows gross loss or debit balance:

Profit and Loss Account Dr.

To Trading Account.

Explanation of the Entry. The trading account shows gross loss or debit balance. In order to close the trading account which shows a debit balance, it should be credited. As the trading account is credited, the profit and loss account to which the balance of the trading account is transferred should be debited.

6. For Closing the Accounts of all Indirect Expenses and Losses: The accounts of all indirect expenses and losses should be closed by transfer to the profit and loss account. For closing the accounts of all indirect expenses and losses, only one closing entry is passed. The entry passed for closing the accounts of all indirect expenses and losses is:

Profit and Loss Account Dr.

To Individual Indirect Expense Account.

Types of Assets and Liabilities Included in a Balance Sheet

As it has been seen earlier, a Balance Sheet is a statement of. assets and liabilities. So it is essential to know something about assets and liabilities.

Assets include all the properties possessed by a concern and all the debts, *i.e.*, amounts due to a concern from other parties.

Assets of a concern may be broadly divided into three classes, *viz.*, (1) fixed assets, (2) fluctuating, floating, circulating or current assets and (3) fictitious assets.

Fixed assets are those assets with the help of which the business is carried on. They are permanently used in the business for the purpose of earning incomes. They are not meant for resale. Examples of fixed assets are lands, buildings, machinery, furniture, motor vehicles, etc.

Floating or fluctuating assets are those which are held temporarily for resale or for immediate conversion into cash or which frequently undergo changes. Examples of floating assets are stock, debtors, bills receivable, cash, etc.

Fictitious assets are those assets which are not represented by any concrete or tangible property. They are generally expenses and losses not written off but carried forward to the subsequent period. Examples of fictitious assets are advertising suspense (*i.e.* advertising expenditure not written off but carried forward to the subsequent period), preliminary expenses (*i.e.* expenses to establish a joint stock company), etc.

Liabilities represent the amounts owing by the business to other parties. The capital of the proprietor is also regarded as a liability because the business owes this amount to the proprietor.

Liabilities may be broadly divided into two classes, *viz.*, (1) fixed liabilities and (2) fluctuating or current liabilities.

Fixed liabilities are those liabilities which will be repaid after a long period of time. They include long-term loans taken from others and the capital belonging to the proprietor.

Current liabilities are those liabilities which have to be repaid immediately or in the near future, usually within a year. They include bank overdraft, sundry creditors, bills payable, outstanding liabilities for expenses, etc.

Arrangement of Assets and Liabilities in the Balance Sheet

The assets and liabilities of a business must be arranged (or shown) in the Balance Sheet in some form. The arrangement of assets and liabilities is called the "marshalling" or "grouping" of assets and liabilities.

The assets of a business can be arranged in the Balance Sheet in two ways, *viz.*, (1) in the order of liquidity or realisability, and (2) in the order of permanence. According to the first method, the assets are arranged in the order in which they can be converted into cash. The assets which can be easily converted into cash come first, and the assets which cannot be easily realised come next. According to the second method, the assets are arranged in the order of permanence. The most fixed assets come first and the assets which change frequently come next.

The liabilities of a business are also arranged in two ways, *viz.*, (1) in the order of dischargeability or payment and (2) in the order of permanence. According to the first method, the liabilities are shown in the order of payment. The liabilities which are payable immediately or in the near future come first, and the liabilities which are payable after a long time come next. According to the second method, the liabilities are shown in the order of permanence. The most fixed liabilities come first, and the immediately payable liabilities come next.

With regard to the arrangement of assets, and liabilities, it should be noted that the same order of arrangement should be followed for both assets and liabilities. If the assets are arranged in the order of realisability, the liabilities should be arranged in the order of payment. If the assets are arranged in the order of permanence, the liabilities also should be arranged in the order of permanence.

The order of realisability of assets and the payment of liabilities is followed by sole-trading concerns and partnership firms. The order of permanence of assets and liabilities is followed by joint stock companies.

If the assets are arranged in the order of realisability, and if the liabilities are arranged in the order of payment, then the assets and liabilities will appear in the Balance Sheet as follows:

Balance Sheet as at ....

Liabilities	*Rs.*	*Assets*	*Rs.*
Bank Overdraft	.....	Cash in Hand	.....
Bills Payable	.....	Cash at Bank	.....
Sundry Creditors	.....	Investments	.....
Liabilities for Expenses	.....	Bills Receivable	.....
Incomes received in advance	.....	Sundry Debtors	.....
Long-term loans	.....	Closing Stock	.....
Capital	.....	Loose Tools	.....
		Furniture and Fixtures	.....
		Plant and Machinery	.....
		Land and Buildings	.....
		Goodwill	.....
	.....		.....

If the assets and liabilities are arranged in the order of pennanence, they will appear as follows:

Balance Sheet as at ......

Liabilities	*Rs.*	*Assets*	*Rs.*
Capital	.....	Goodwill	.....
Long-term loans	.....	Land and Buildings	.....
Incomes received in advance	.....	Plant and Machinery	.....
Liabilities for expenses	.....	Furniture and Fixtures	.....

Contd.

Liabilities	*Rs.*	*Assets*	*Rs.*
Sundry Creditors	.....	Loose Tools	.....
Bills Payable	.....	Closing Stock	.....
Bank Overdraft	.....	Sundry Debtors	.....
		Bills Receivable	.....
		Investments	.....
		Cash at Bank	.....
		Cash in Hand	.....
	.....		.....

Valuation of Assets. We have studied earlier that the object of a Balance Sheet is to show the true financial position of the business as on a particular date. For this purpose, the assets shown in the Balance Sheet must be properly valued. The following is the rule for the valuation of assets:

Fixed Assets. As the fixed assets are held for the purpose of use in the business, they must be valued on the basis of their usefulness to the business, *i.e.* at cost price less reasonable depreciation.

Floating Assets. As the floating assets are held for the purpose of resale, they must be valued on the basis of their realisa bility, *i.e.* at cost price or market price, whichever is lower.

The following illustrations will show how adjusting and closing entries are passed and final accounts are prepared.

Illustration 1.

The following are some of the balances extracted from the Ledger of Srikanth as on 31 st December, 2000. Prepare a Trading Account.

		Rs.	Rs.
Stock	—	12,500	
Purchases	—	78,000	
Sales	—		1,25,000
Returns Outwards	—		3,000
Returns Inwards	—	5,000	
Salaries	—	4,400	
Wages	—	7,500	
Rent	—	2,750	
Carriage Inwards	—	2,500	
Carriage Outwards	—	750	

Stock on 31-12-2000 was valued at Rs. 14,000.

Solution.

Srikanth
Trading Account
For the year ended 31st December, 2000

Dr. Cr.

	Rs.	Rs.		Rs.	Rs.
To Opening Stock		12,500	By Sales	1,25,000	
To Purchases	78,000		*Less* : Sales Returns	5,000	1,20,000
Less: Purchases Returns	3,000	75,000	By Closing Stock		14,000
To Wages	7,500				
To Carriage Inwards	2.500				
To Gross Profit (Transferred to P & L A/c)	36,500	46,500			
		1,34,000			1,34,000

Note: Salaries, Rent and Carriage outwards—these items are Indirect Expenses. They will not be shown in the Trading Account. Such expenses are shown in the Profit and Loss Account on the debit side.

12

Instructor and Lesson Planning

The success or failure of any educational programme depends upon the quality of instruction. Besides courses of study, reading material, equipment and good spacious classrooms, good supervision and administration also contribute to the success and effectiveness of instruction. All these factors are ineffective without a good teacher who possesses certain qualities of head and heart. To quote *Sir John Adams*, "If the teacher is to prove really a maker of man, he must possess qualities of personality, character and intellect". However, the teacher has got his own limitations. All the teachers of Commerce may not possess all the required qualities but they should try to equip themselves with the maximum possible qualities in spite of their own limitations.

1. Physical Qualities

(i) Good Personal Appearance. A teacher should have a good personal appearance to produce good impression upon those who come in his contact. Free from all physical deformities and abnormalities, he should be neither too tall nor too short, neither too fleshy nor too lean, neither too black nor too white. He should be a normal human being having tolerable features, smart, clever and active. A shabbily dressed, untidy and bad-looking teacher is seldom liked and owned by the pupils.

(ii) *Clear and Pleasant Voice.* A commerce teacher should possess a clear appealing voice, neither too low nor unnecessarily loud and shrill. Regular practice and care can make his voice effective and appealing. He should neither shout in the class nor speak too fast. Clear in his speech he should be audible to all of his pupils, sitting in different corners of the classroom.

(iii) *Good Physical Health.* Physical health brings smartness, enthusiam, vigour, vitality, and activeness, so essential for a Commerce teacher. Good physical health will make the teacher alert, cheerful and emotionally stable enabling him to meet the day-to-day demands of a modern school. A sound mind can live only in a sound body. A sound body requires regularity and moderation of habits, simple nourishing diet, participation in sports and games and physical exercise.

2. Moral Qualities

(i) *Friendliness, Sympathy and Understanding.* A good teacher should be the best friend and guide of his pupils. Sympathetic, kind hearted and humane towards his pupils he must understand their difficulties and problems and try to remove them. As pupils look to him for guidance and encouragement at every step, he must exhibit deep interest in them, in their activities, their welfare and their progress in studies.

(ii) *Honesty, Sincerity and Impartiality.* Absolutely fair in his dealings with others, a good teacher must be just, honest and impartial and free from all prejudices and bias. To win respect from others his words must reflect his actions. As *M.K.Gandhi* said, "Woe to the teacher who teaches one thing with the lips and carries another in the heart." Not the teacher's words, but his actions carry weight with the young students.

3. Psychological Qualities

(i) ***Tactullness, Patience and Self-control.*** A good Commerce teacher should do the right thing at the right moment, even under trying circumstances. He should be able to skilfully control the young children under his charge. He must keep cool and balanced. He should exhibit patience and control of nerves even if things are not happening according to his wishes and expectations. Patience is required not only dealing with own pupils but also with officials senior colleagues, publicmen and common people.

(ii) ***A Sense of Humour.*** "The classroom has no place for a confirmed pessimist and long faced, sour-visaged and humourless grouch. The classroom needs to be a happy place and it cannot be that without a good-natured teacher in charge." Therefore a good teacher should possess a sense of humour to delight his pupils in tense moments. A good laugh will relax pent-up feelings and exhausted nerves and will, thus, pave a way for further action and concentrated efforts.

(iii) ***Sound Mental Health.*** A dejected, frustrated, melancholic and pessimist teacher cannot create wholesome influence upon his pupils. He must always be cheerful and optimist and have faith in the goodness of humanity. Whatever may be the conditions and circumstances in which he is put, he must adjust himself to those environments. This is possible only when he possesses emotional stability and control over his anger and passions.

4. Executive Qualities

(i) ***Initiative and Resourcefulness.*** A good teacher should be able to collect material and adopt his plans according to the circumstances. He should be sensible enough to take independent action in case of emergency as and when the occasion demands. Without running to the Headmaster or to other superior officers, he should be able to fare problems, think of their solution and then try to solve them to the best of his ability.

(ii) ***Organising and Directive Capacity.*** As an organiser, the commerce teacher should be able to put his plans into a workable form. For a job to be done in the best possible manner and with the least wastage of time, money and energy. He should select the most competent person for doing a job for which he or she is best fitted and in which he or she is genuinely interested. He should chalk out plans and prepare a framework before hand to facilitate the desired educational programme. As a leader and a director, he must be a person of wisdom and vision, with a thorough knowledge of facts.

5. Scholarship. Scholarship is not only desirable but essential for a successful Commerce teacher, the subject, he is required to teach, is very vast and extensive. He may be face to face with many problems, if his own knowledge is not broader than the subject-matter that he teaches. In ancient India a teacher was held in high esteem in society because of his scholarship and high degree of learning the Commerce teacher must have:

(i) ***A Sound Knowledge of the Subject-matter.*** A Commerce teacher must know his subject well enough and deep enough. To have a broad and thorough knowledge of the content fields to enable him to

select material for his subject according to his needs. He must be a specialist in at least two of the Social Sciences such as history, geography, economics, political science and sociology.

(ii) ***Originality.*** A regular reader of books, newspapers, periodicals and magazines etc. should keep his knowledge thorough and up-to-date. Commerce teacher should not be contented only by what others say but should be in a position to form his own independent judgement of men and affairs. He should have a habit of enquiry and scientific approach, desire for truth and spirit of independence, and initiative and originality to face any classroom situation that may arise unexpectedly

(iii) ***A Background of General and Liberal Education.*** The commerce teacher must be broad and of varied interests. He must apply his mind in as many subjects and activities as possible. He should have a keen interest in current affairs, an appreciation for the dominant role of science in human life and a habit of approaching social problems with the scientific method of enquiry. He should be able to explain the present in relation to the past correctly and successfully. He should keep himself very well-informed about all the happenings and general problems concerning men and affairs.

6. Professional Background. Professional background is also essential for successful teaching. Professional background includes:

(i) ***Professional Attitude.*** A real teacher is not a person who merely takes up a teaching job. He becomes a teacher by his faith and mental attitude. Possessing a natural aptitude for this profession, he takes to teaching, not because nothing else was available to

him to make both ends meet, but because he was fired with the ambition of serving humanity through a vocation of his own liking and interest. He looks upon his work as a sort of dedication and mission not as a job or profession.

(ii) Desire for Improvement. Teaching is a progressive occupation A teacher must always be a student. He must keep himself abreast of the latest development through regular study of books, newspapers, journals and magazines etc. He must be able to understand the perplexing problems of present-day world in their true context. He should know that education is dynamic and not static. He should always strive for improvement. Besides reading latest books and magazines on education, he should also attend seminars, refresher courses meetings, conferences, and work-shops on this subject, held in each state under Extension Services Department, attached to Teachers Training Colleges.

(iii) Processional Training. A good teacher must undergo professional training as teaching is both an art and a science. Like all other technical professions teaching requires sound professional training. A Commerce teacher must, attend a full course of training in a teachers training college. During which he will study effective methodical procedures as well as proper use of audio-visual aids. He will also study child psychology to understand the chief mental and physical characteristics of the various stages of the child's development.

7. Good Relationship

(i) Relationship with Pupils. To command faith, loyalty and respect a teacher must take genuine interest in his pupils. He must mix with them, play with them, participate in various activities and encourage them on all occasions. He must pay individual attention towards the backward, abnormal and problem students.

(ii) Relationship with Community. A teacher should feel himself responsible to the whole society. The school is an agency that society has set up to instruct its young members. He, therefore, has an obligation to the parents of his pupils and to the community at large. As both home and school are engaged in a cooperative task we must, welcome contacts and conferences with parents on various occasions in the interest of the education of this pupils.

(iii) Relationship with Colleagues. The teacher must cultivate intimate relationship. With other members of the staff he must always be obliging and co-operating. He must give his colleagues a helping hand whenever required. He must neither backbite nor unnecessarily interfere in their affairs. He should work closely with the administration and be obedient and loyal. He should, enjoy academic freedom, but not do anything that will reflect upon his position as a teacher.

Lesson Planning

The word meaning of 'lesson planning' means to plan to lesson so as to attain educational objectives. The teaching process has to pass through three phases:

(a) Pre-active phase

(b) Inter-active phase

(c) Post-active phase

The lesson planning is concerned with pre-active phase of teaching. In this phase, the teacher has to plan different activities relating to teaching. So, in simple words, to write down systematically all those activities which he will carry out in the class to attain instructional objectives, is known as lesson planning.

According to *Davis*, "Lesson plan must be prepared before going to the class, for there is nothing so fatal to a teacher's progress as unpreparedness."

According to *N.L. Bossin*, "Lesson-plan is the title given to a statement: of achievements to be realised and the specific means by which these are attained as a result of activities engaged during the period."

In brief, we can say that careful planning of lesson is essential for good teaching. Ryburn said, "To teach, we must use experiences already gained as starting point of our work."

As in other subjects, in teaching Commerce too, the teacher must keep in mind the following facts:

(i) To state the objectives of teaching in broad terms.

(ii) After stating broad teaching objectives, those should be precisely deemed and specified in behavioural terms.

(iii) To organise the subject matter for realising set objectives.

(iv) To arrange re-inforcement, for evaluation of teaching learning.

Need and Importance of Lesson Planning

Lesson planning is necessary for successful teaching. The lesson plan covers, the sort of questions to be asked to arouse curiosity of pupils, and to overcome their difficulties. So, with pre-planning, he finds himself capable of achieving aims of teaching adequately. The following is the importance and the need of lesson planning.

1. **Organisation of Subject-matter.** For achieving the set objectives it is necessary to organise the subject-matter. The importance of lesson planning is there for presenting the subject-matter and its evaluation.

2. **Clarity of Teaching Objectives.** For the clarity of objectives of teaching, he does not waste time by going astray. It is because the objectives will be clear.

3. **Knowledge of Teaching Activities.** Before writing the lesson plan the teacher decides teaching activities and how to use teaching aids.

4. **Organised Knowledge.** It is necessary to present the knowledge to the pupils in an organised form. This makes their learning more effective.

5. **Dreaming Objectives.** For teaching a subject, lesson planning is necessary, to define the objectives, offer a norm for organising and evacuating the subject-matter.

6. **Knowledge of Problems.** Through the medium of lesson planning, the teacher thinks out the problems and difficulties relating to the lesson and how to solve them.

7. **Development of Mental Power.** The lesson plan helps in developing reasoning, decision making, imagination in the pupils.

8. **Utility of Individual Differences.** Keeping individual differences of the pupils in mind, he can prepare various kinds of lesson plans.

9. **To Establish Relationship between Teaching and Learning.** Through lesson planning practical relationship can be established between teaching and learning. In education, close relationship.

between teaching and learning is very necessary. So, for this purpose lesson planning is helpful.

10. **For Reinforcement.** Through lesson planning the teacher decides pupils activities and the situations for using devices for reinforcement.

11. **For Interesting Teaching.** To make lesson interesting, clear and simple, it is necessary to select in advance, the relevant methods, devices and strategies. To achieve this aim, the teacher must prepare the lesson plan before hand.

12. **To Control Indiscipline.** At times, the cause of indiscipline in the class, is lack of preparation on the part of the teacher. So planning of lesson is important and essential for handling such problems.

13. **New Knowledge on the Basis of Previous Knowledge.** In the lesson plan, new knowledge is given on the basic of previous knowledge. This accounts for newness and simplification of the lesson. All activities, of class level and suitable to syllabus, are selected in advance. This creates interest of the students in the lesson.

14. **To Provide Outline.** In teacher training, the lesson plan presents the outline of the class activities.

Thus we see, how important and necessary is lesson planning in modern age. On psychological grounds too, lesson plan offers moral strength to the teacher. So, before going to the class the teacher should prepare the lesson plan.

Preparation of Lesson Plan

Educational world and teacher under training are highly indebted to the great educationist *Herbart*, a leading exponent of psychological tendencies in education for his Five Harbartian

Steps. According to him teaching is not a right process. It depends more on the resourcefullness and way of handling of the subject-matter by the teacher of Commerce than the application of the old orthodox and conservative educational, principles or doctrines. But a few general principles for preparing it lesson-plan can briefly be laid down for the guidance of the young under-trainees.

(a) A lesson plan should always be drawn psychologically.

(b) It should be arranged properly, sub-headings should be mentioned briefly and specifically.

(c) While drawing a lesson plan in commerce or social sciences a teacher should take advantage of the different maxims of teaching like from known to unknown, from particular to general, from concrete to abstract and from immediate to the remote or from the present to the past, etc.

(d) A lesson of history plan should have the accurate consideration of time and space whereas a lesson of geography should have, accurate consideration of cause and effect. If stories whether of history or geography are selected at junior stage, they should be arranged in chronological order.

(e) It is always advisable to divide the lesson plan into different units. Each unit should be given the up-to-date treatment it deserves.

These steps start after we have fulfilled the formal blackboard entries like, class, subject, topic, time, period and average age of the students.

1. General Aims. General aims of various branches of Commerce more or less remain the same. Following may be stated briefly as the general aims of commerce.

(a) To let the students understand the evolutionary process of growth of human society.

(b) To develop the power of imagination, reasoning and judgement through the teaching of Commerce.

(c) Enrichment and development of the lives of the pupils in their natural and social environment.

(d) To make the students intelligent, patriotic and also to develop a cosmopolitan outlook in the students *i.e.* socialisation of students and promotion of international understanding.

(e) To prepare the students for the future. To make them familiar with the present as the outcome of the past. It means let them understand the experiences of the race.

(f) Formation of habits and skills.

(g) Training in desirable pattern of conduct.

It is not necessary that all the aims stated above can be achieved in a lesson but the teacher has to strived realise as many aims as is possible in various lessons.

2. Specific Aim. The specific aim is concerned with the topic of the lesson. It should be written quite particularly and clearly. It should give the idea of what the teacher actually wants to achieve with the teaching of that topic. The specific aim, it should be borne in mind, should never be long and complex.

3. Material Aid. Material aid is needed to create an effective atmosphere in the teaching of the lesson. But it is not necessarily essential to produce it in every lesson. The following qualities of a good material aid should be borne in mind while selecting them.

(i) It should be relevant to the topic under discussion.

(ii) It should be produced at the proper time when the lesson is going on.

(iii) It is better to draw diagrams, sketch, maps on the blackboard and in the presence of the students.

(iv) It should not be too costly.

(v) The teacher should make a proper arrangement for the production of the material. If pictures and models are used, they should not be removed immediately. Let the students should form their impression in their mind.

4. Previous Knowledge Assumed. A teacher should be very careful in his assumption of the previous knowledge. The introduction of the new lesson will depend on a correct assumption of the previous knowledge. It can make the effectiveness of the introductory stage.

5. Introduction. This is indeed the beginning of the lesson. This is a stage with its unique importance. Well begun is half done holds true in this case. Following are the aims of introductory stage.

Aims

(a) To create an effective atmosphere for the teaching of the new lesson.

(b) To test the previous knowledge.

(c) To create preparedness in the students for the reception of the new knowledge.

What should be the Qualities of a Good Introduction?

(a) It should be neither too long nor too short, four to six questions are sufficient.

(*b*) All the questions should have psychological arrangements.

(*c*) It should not be vague and indefinite.

(*d*) It should be based upon the previous knowledge assumed.

At the stage of introduction, the teacher should have the performance like a juggler. Juggler seldom starts the demonstration of his feats unless he has been able to catch the attention of his spectators. A teacher should consider his introductory task successful, only when he has been able to develop curiosity among the pupils at this stage. The success of the lesson to a large extent depends upon the successful performance of the introductory stage.

6. Statement of Aim. After the introductory work is over, the teacher should give the statement of aim. The statement of the aim should have the following questions:

(*a*) It should be explained strictly the aim of that particular lesson. It should not be vague and indefinite.

(*b*) It should be emphasised the utility of that particular lesson in the present day.

(*c*) It should be brief and well wooded. It is not sufficient to state that "Today, we shall read about Ashoka but a good form of it would be Today we shall try to be familiar with the significant reign of Ashoka whose integrity, piety and devotion to duty has affected the modern society of ours."

7. Presentation. This is a stage for the transmission of the new knowledge to the students. The stage of presentation does not present such a great difficulty in the language lesson as in case of Social sciences such as geography, economics, civics and history, The following points should be taken into consideration at the stage of presentation of Commerce lesson:

(a) It should be divided into units. It is always better to divide the stage of presentation into two or three units.

(b) The presentation is to be divided into two parts *i.e.,* Matter and Method plus expected answers from the students.

(c) A few questions should be put to the students to test and develop the time-sense of the students.

(d) The subject-matter should be arranged in a chronological manner.

(e) Use of regressive method should be made whenever and wherever it is possible.

(f) There should be psychological link between questions. Where psychological link is not possible because of dissimilarity between the nature of two questions, they should be connected with the intervening statement of the teacher. One question should lead the other.

(g) It is always better to develop the presentation in the form of questions in order to secure more cooperation of the class.

(h) The presents should be linked with the past whenever and wherever it is possible.

(i) The following types of question should be avoided.

  (a) Questions of complex nature.

  (b) Questions not properly wonded.

  (c) Suggestive questions.

(d) Questions have answers in the form of 'yes.' or 'no'.

(e) Abstract questions.

(j) Questions should be thought provoking.

(k) Whenever and wherever it is possible, generalisation should be drawn.

(l) The form of question should not be changed very often otherwise the students can get confused. If need be, the form or question can be changed when the teacher is satisfied that a slight change in the form may help in eliciting quick response from the students.

(m) Lastly, presentation should suit the mental level and academic standard of the students for whom it is meant.

8. Black-Board Summary. It is an index of teacher's work with the class. Following points may be specified here for guidance in this respect:

(i) Preferably, Black-Board summary should be developed along with the lesson.

(ii) Complex sentences should be avoided. It should merely be develop in main and significant points.

(iii) It should be a summary of the lesson and not supplementary to it.

(iv) Black-Board handwriting should be neat, bold and uniform.

9. Home-Task. A teacher should give a proper thought before it is assigned to the class. Before he assigns home-task he should bear the following points in mind:

(i) Its main objective is to use properly the leisure time of the students.

(ii) It should be given in coordination with other subject teacher.

(iii) It should have variety *i.e.* long answer types, short answer types, objective types, filling the gap, preparation of diagram, maps, or if possible, making of models.

Advantages of Lesson Planning

1. Planning of a lesson helps the teacher to organise his teaching thoroughly.
2. The teacher of Commerce is clear about the knowledge already gained by the students and what more he is expected to teach them.
3. By doing so teaching becomes more clear and effective.
4. The information about the topic is imparted to the students step by step and not in a haphazard manner.
5. With lesson planning sequence of the information supplied about various facts is maintained.
6. Lesson plan helps to link the old knowledge with new one.
7. The sectional/partial recapitulation is very necessary if the lesson in Commerce, is long. This step is for reinforcement of knowledge.

Herbartian Approach of Lesson Plan

Taking the five steps of *Herbart*, as the base, the following steps of the lesson plan can be set. Following these, pupil-teachers can write their own lesson plans.

(i) **Subject, Topic, Class, Section, Period and Date.** The lesson plan is prepared, after deciding these points. According to the subject, choice is made of the topic, and sub-topic.

(ii) **General Objectives.** His necessary to set some general aims to back the lesson. The success of teaching depends upon achieving these objectives. Evaluation of teachers teaching is also done with reference to these general objectives.

(iii) **Teaching Aids.** The teacher has to decide about the aids to be used in the lesson *e.g.* the use of the black-board, model/chart, radio/tape recorder projector, television etc.

(iv) **Specific Aim.** This objective is based on the central theme of the lesson. It is fixed up on the basis of the subject-matter.

(v) **Previous Knowledge.** In teaching, it is necessary to think about previous knowledge. So as to teach new knowledge. For teaching new knowledge, the previous knowledge acts as its base.

(vi) **Introduction.** It is based on the previous knowledge of the pupils. The new lesson is reached through the medium of the introduction. This step, in the lesson plan is considered as very important. For introduction, questions are asked on previous knowledge, to link with the new topic: For this he puts three to four questions, so that the proposed topic may be linked with the previous knowledge.

(vii) **Presentation.** The practical part of the lesson begins with presentation. At this stage, the teacher must motivate the pupils. Questions are put in this step for the progress of the lesson.

(viii) **Statement of Aim.** The teacher, relating to the topic, announces that we shall study this topic today.

(ix) **Home-Work.** The importance of home-work, in teaching is second to none. So, the home-task must be given. Different types of questions can be given in home-task step.

(x) **Recapitulation.** To revise the lesson taught is called recapitulation. This enables one to know, about the success of the lesson. With getting correct answers of recapitulatory questions the success of teaching can be guessed. If the lesson is divided into units, then after every unit, revision should be there.

(xi) **Black-Board Summary.** The teacher writes the teaching points on the black-board. The black-board happens to be his friend. Without this, the teacher cannot be successful. The black-board summary should be written simultaneously or after the teacher's narration is over.

(xii) **Clarification.** On getting no reply to these developmental questions, the teacher himself offers explanation so that there remains no doubt or conflict in the minds of the pupils.

Merits of Herbartian Approach

1. It is based upon psychological principles.
2. Its nature is, well organised and well controlled.
3. It can be used for all subjects.
4. It is powerful for bringing unconscious thoughts to conscious mind.
5. Its use simplifies lesson planning task.

6. It uses Inductive and Deductive methods.
7. It is based upon previously learned knowledge.
8. It teaches how to use the newly learned knowledge in new situations.
9. The pupils are active and get opportunities to think originally.
10. All knowledge is gained in a coordinated manner.

emerits of Herbartian Approach

1. There is more emphasis on presentation.
2. Teacher's freedom is limited.
3. With this approach only knowledge lessons can be taught effectively, whereas for skill and appreciation lessons it is not suitable.
4. The lesson plan is less flexible.
5. Less attention is paid to pupils interests and aptitudes.
6. Teaching comes to memory level.
7. Teaching objectives and learning conditions are not kept under considerations.
8. In the lesson plan the specification of teaching objectives is not done.

Characteristics of Good Lesson Plan

The lesson plan should have the following characteristics:

- It should be written.
- It should be related to previous knowledge.
- Adequate care should be there in the selection of subject-matter.

- It should explicitly mention general and specific objectives.
- There should be clear indication of activities involved in the lesson.
- Should be based on individual differences.
- Should be related to life situations.
- It should be based upon good teaching methods.
- It should be suitable to the child's interests, tendencies, capabilities and aptitudes.
- It should make use of examples and aids so that the lesson becomes simple, interesting and easily comprehensible.
- It should have provision for the pupils to choose activities and scope for guidance.
- It should give expected space to every point.
- It should give room for assignments.
- It should have place for criticism of the lesson.
- Should mention home-task.
- Should be divided into units.
- It should be neat and clean, beautiful.

The lesson plan is a servant and not the master of the teacher. He should be active throughout the lesson. Having decided the teachers and pupils activities, the plan should be flexible as to permit the teacher to make change as per conditions to cope up and to leave no scope for going astray, so that the majority of pupils may take full interest in the lesson.

Index

Q

R

S

T

U

V

W

More Titles are Available in

TEXT BOOKS

1.	Advanced Educational Psycology **(New)**	175/-
2.	Educational Administration & Origanisational Management **(New)**	195/-
3.	Social Psycology **(New)**	225/-
4.	Teaching of commerce **(New)**	175/-
5.	Educational Development & Technology **(New)**	175/-
6.	Disaster Management **(New)**	175/-
7.	Information Technology **(New)**	225/-
8.	Human Resource Development **(New)**	175/-
9.	Mass Media Communication **(New)**	225/-
10.	Adult Education **(New)**	175/-
11.	General Psychology **(New)**	175/-
12.	Distance Education **(New)**	175/-
13.	Teachers Education **(New)**	175/-
14.	Educational Philosophy **(New)**	175/-
15.	Science Teaching in Schools **(New)**	150/-
16.	Teaching of Chemistry **(New)**	175/-
17.	Modern Education for New Generation **(New)**	175/-
18.	Indian Polity **(Revised New)**	295/-
19.	New Comparative Government **(Revised New)**	275/-
	Advance Study in the History of Modern India (PB)	
20.	(Volume-1: 1707-1803)	195/-
21.	(Volume-2: 1803-1920)	295/-
22.	(Volume-3: 1920-1947)	135/-
23.	Handbook of Nutrition & Dietetics **(New)**	250/-
24.	Development of Education in India	175/-
25.	A Text Book of Environmental Studies	175/-
26.	Teaching of History	175/-

27. Administrative Thinkers 175/-
28. Research Methodology 175/-
29. Curriculum Development 195/-
30. Teaching of Science 160
31. Teaching of Mathematics 160/-
32. Principles of Educational & Vocational guidance 175/-
33. Child Psychology 175/-
34. Abnormal Psychology 175/-
35. Indian Education in Emerging Society 175/-
36. Human Resource Management 160/-
37. Higher Education and Global Challenges 175/-
38. Teaching of Geography 150/-
39. Teaching of Social Studies 150/-
40. Teaching of English 175/-
41. Principles of Office Management **(Revised Ed.)** 250/-
42. Education for All: The Indian Saga 175/-
43. Value Education in Global Perspective 175/-
44. Teacher Training 150/-
45. Public Administration 150/-
46. Public Relations & Integrated Communications 195/-
47. Educational Psychology 150/-
48. Introduction to Educational Technology 175/-
49. Textbook of Food and Nutrition 150/-